**Distinctly Asian,
Unmistakably World Class**

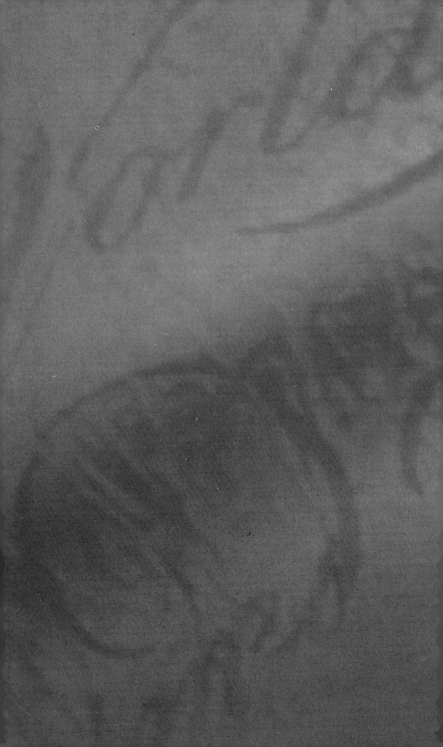

Tiger Beer

**Distinctly Asian,
Unmistakably World Class**

Jacky Tai

mc Marshall Cavendish
Business

Text copyright © 2008 Jacky Tai
Image on page 24: British Crown Copyright
All other images courtesy of Asia Pacific Breweries Ltd

Project team: Lee Mei Lin and Lock Hong Liang

First published in 2008 by:
Marshall Cavendish Business
An imprint of Marshall Cavendish International
1 New Industrial Road
Singapore 536196
T: +65 6213 9300 / F: +65 6285 4871
E: genref@sg.marshallcavendish.com
Online bookstore: www.marshallcavendish.com/genref

and

Cyan Communications Limited
5th Floor
32–38 Saffron Hill
London EC1N 8FH
United Kingdom
T: +44 (0)20 7565 6120 / F: +44 (0)20 7734 6221 / www.cyanbooks.com

Other Marshall Cavendish Offices:
Marshall Cavendish Ltd. 5th Floor, 32–38 Saffron Hill, London EC1N 8FH, UK • Marshall Cavendish Corporation. 99 White Plains Road, Tarrytown NY 10591-9001, USA • Marshall Cavendish International (Thailand) Co Ltd. 253 Asoke, 12th Flr, Sukhumvit 21 Road, Klongtoey Nua, Wattana, Bangkok 10110, Thailand • Marshall Cavendish (Malaysia) Sdn Bhd, Times Subang, Lot 46, Subang Hi-Tech Industrial Park, Batu Tiga, 40000 Shah Alam, Selangor Darul Ehsan, Malaysia

Marshall Cavendish is a trademark of Times Publishing Limited

National Library Board Singapore Cataloguing in Publication Data
Tai, Jacky, 1970-
Tiger Beer : distinctly Asian, unmistakably world class / Jacky Tai. – Singapore : Marshall Cavendish Business, 2008.
p. cm. – (Great Asian brands)
ISBN-13 : 978-981-261-845-0
ISBN-10 : 981-261-845-7

1. Beer – Singapore – Marketing. 2. Brand name products – Singapore. 3. Branding (Marketing) – Singapore. I. Title. II. Series: Great Asian brands

HD69.B7
658.827095957 -- dc22   OCN179767073

Printed in Singapore by Times Graphics Pte Ltd

contents

acknowledgements

This book is made possible thanks to the contributions of all the people at Asia Pacific Breweries, especially the champions of the Tiger Beer brand. They are the ones who have made the Tiger Beer brand the icon that it is today.

Thank you and keep up the great work, folks!

foreword

If you have ever wanted to be a fly on the wall in a major Singapore marketing organisation, this is your book. It is a must-read book for all local brand owners aspiring to grow their brands regionally and globally, and a superb sourcebook for all students of marketing and advertising. Significantly, it is one of those rare marketing volumes that is not afraid to tell the truth and drag the skeletons, kicking and screaming, from the closet.

After Singapore Airlines, Tiger Beer is arguably Singapore's second most famous and iconic brand. In this book, the brand is placed under author Jacky Tai's intrepid magnifying glass. Tai, an accomplished marketer and brand consultant, charts the brand's growth and explores its successes and failures with uncommon warts-and-all candour.

He is a passionate advocate of consistency in branding and communications. He provides invaluable evidence of Tiger Beer's success under the consistent "Good as Gold" theme. He shares the nuances of Tiger Beer's branding strategies, casts light on its brand communications failures, and digs into the problems of retaining brand communications control and consistency in diverse export markets. He probes the global future for the brand, shares the brand's usual market entry process, and takes us behind the scenes of Tiger Beer's forays into foreign markets such as Vietnam. (These hard-won lessons alone make the price of the book a bargain.)

Tai's frank and passionate advice underpins every chapter, and the lessons we can draw from this book are invaluable. One of my favourites is: "A weak brand is usually weak because it tries to be everything to everyone." Amen to that. It's the kind of sage, timeless brand-building advice that is all too frequently forgotten when a brand is being pecked to death by ducks, most of whom are on the company payroll.

Jim Aitchison
Former executive creative director of Batey Ads Group, Singapore, and author of *How Asia Advertises*, *Cutting Edge Advertising* and *Cutting Edge Commercials*

introduction

When the business community in Singapore, and Asia for that matter, talk about successful brands that they can emulate, the tendency is usually to look at examples from the West. And this is something that many entrepreneurs have lamented to me. A typical comment goes like this: "All these Western brands, yes, they are successful but we don't relate to them so well. We want to see local brands but there just aren't any we can draw inspiration from. And don't you name government-linked corporations to us. They are in a different class altogether. We can't do what they do."

Well, here's some good news. This book is about Tiger Beer, one of Singapore's most iconic brands and a brand that has put Singapore on the world map. In a short period of time, Tiger Beer has managed to etch itself into the minds of beer drinkers in the West as a premium and exotic beer from Asia. This is no mean feat as the Western beer market is highly competitive with many strong and entrenched players. How did Tiger Beer do it? How did this brew from the little red dot that is Singapore—a country that is known more for its chilli crabs than for beer—manage to thrive despite its obvious heritage handicap?

This book will give you an insight into how Tiger Beer has done it, so that you can draw inspiration from the ways of the Tiger Beer—from how it formed successful strategic alliances to its brand strategy, marketing tactics, advertising campaigns and everything else in between.

But before we go into that, let's take a light-hearted look into this fascinating brew called beer. Since the beginning of time, humankind has been trying to nail down the differences between men and women, not just in terms of the obvious physiological differences but more in the unseen aspects, such as how men and women think and perceive things. From my own unscientific observations over the years, I can surmise that the only difference between men and women is this—beer. That's right. Beer. How so?

Have you ever paid attention to how guys and girls deal with break-ups? It's really interesting. If a woman just went through a break-up with a man she thought was the one, her girlfriends will try to comfort her and talk things over with her. "Oh, honey, I'm so sorry to hear about the news. You want to talk about it? You'll feel better." And they will talk about it till the moon turns blue. But when a guy shares the same news with his other guy friends and says he's feeling down in the dumps, they will probably say: "I see. That's tough, man. Come on, let's go out and have a beer."

I know, I know. My so-called theory is superficial but that aside, you cannot deny that beer is something that is integral in most people's lives, and not just the men's. Of course, there are light drinkers and heavy drinkers but almost everyone you know drinks beer, even if it is only occasionally.

Beer is one of the oldest beverages in the world. In fact, the earliest known chemical evidence of beer dates back to between 3500 and 3100 BC. Researchers from the University of Pennsylvania's Applied Science Center for Archaeology (MASCA) at The University Museum of Archaeology and Anthropology analysed an organic residue from inside a clay vessel found in the Zagros Mountains of western Iran and found what is the earliest chemical evidence of beer.[1] Fast forward to 2006. In that year, beer consumption was estimated to be 133 billion litres, which in turn generated revenues of US$295 billion for breweries.[2] That makes beer the most popular alcoholic beverage in the world, way ahead of other popular alcoholic beverages like wine.

Tiger Beer is a lager, which is defined as an effervescent beer that is light in colour and body. 'Lager' is the English name for the bottom fermenting beers (made from bottom fermenting yeast such as *Saccharomyces pastorianus*), and the name comes from the German word *lagern*, which means 'to store'. This beer was first produced in the cellars of eastern European castles and

1. http://www.museum.upenn.edu/new/research/Exp_Res_Disc/mascalheers.html

2. http://www.researchandmarkets.com/reports/53577/beer_global_industry_guide.html

monasteries, where the low winter temperatures were conducive for the lager fermentation. Today, lager is the most commonly consumed type of beer.

The lager yeast typically undergoes primary fermentation at 7 to 12 degrees Celsius (the fermentation phase) and is then given a long secondary fermentation at 0 to 4 degrees Celsius (the lagering phase). It is during the latter stage that the lager clears and mellows. The cooler conditions also inhibit the natural production of esters and other by-products, resulting in a crisp tasting beer. Modern methods of producing lager were pioneered by Gabriel Sedlmayr the Younger, who perfected dark brown lagers at the Spaten Brewery in Bavaria, and Anton Dreher, who began brewing a lager, probably of amber red colour, in Vienna in the early 1840s. With improved modern yeast strains, most lager breweries use only short periods of cold storage that typically last between one and three weeks.

This is all very fascinating, I'm sure, but beer making is not the focus of this book. This book is all about Tiger Beer, and you want to know how it became an iconic Singapore brand that is iconic not only in the island nation but in some of the trendiest bars and pubs in some of the trendiest cities in the world. The year 2007 marked not only Tiger Beer's 75th anniversary but also its foray into its 60th export market, Papua New Guinea. So sit back, relax and enjoy the ride—preferably with an ice cold Tiger Beer in your hand!

1

An Icon Is Born

There
are not many brands in Singapore that can be considered iconic. Tiger Beer, however, is one of them. But it is the most unlikely of brand heroes because Singapore is not a country known for its beer brewing prowess. While other countries like Germany and The Netherlands have been brewing beer for hundreds of years, Singapore's beer brewing history only really started with Tiger Beer in the 20th century. Despite that, Tiger Beer has managed to work its way into the collective psyche of the nation, and against all odds it has even become an international success. How was this iconic Singapore beer born?

Well, on 15 April 1931, a well-known Dutch beer brewery, Heineken, formed a joint venture with a major Singapore soft drinks company, Fraser and Neave Limited. This joint venture company was listed as Malayan Breweries Limited because, at that time, Singapore was still part of Malaya. Heineken had all the necessary technical expertise, having brewed beer since 1873, but it was having difficulty entering the local market. And so it looked to a partnership with a local company, one that had the necessary market knowledge and a strong distribution network. Heineken found the right partner in Fraser and Neave, which also had the necessary capital to build a brewery from the ground up. A deal was made.

That joint venture company eventually became Asia Pacific Breweries Limited (APB), which is a public listed company on the Singapore Exchange. APB is owned by four major shareholders: the investing public (19.7 per cent); Heineken (9.4 per cent); Fraser and Neave (4.8 per cent). The remaining 66.1 per cent is owned by Asia Pacific Investment Pte Ltd, which is in turn a 50/50 joint venture between Heineken and Fraser and Neave.

The first batch of Tiger Beer was brewed on 1 October 1932 at

The original brewery on Alexandra Road, circa 1932. Seated are representatives from Heineken and Fraser and Neave.

the original Tiger Beer brewery on Alexandra Road. That brewery has since given way to a modern high-rise office building where Tiger Beer continues to be headquartered. Tiger Beer was launched with much fanfare on that same day and hundreds of Singaporeans turned up for the momentous event. Watching Tiger Beer being born must have been a proud moment for them because it proved that the little island was capable of doing something that had hitherto been the preserve of the Europeans and Americans. This was what *The Straits Times*, which covered the launch event 76 years ago, said in a report in 1932:

> Over 200 guests attended and they were given as much beer as they desired, and an eloquent tribute to the new beverage lay in the fact that many who were not regular drinkers asked for a second while others had a third.

Top: Another view of the brewery. Bottom: Tiger Beer's launch event in October 1932 attracted over 200 guests.

Well, it looks like Tiger Beer got the taste right from the word go, which is an important thing. In branding, perception is reality, and perception is more important than quality in brand building. But the quality must be at least as good as that of the competitors'. Being the new kid on the block, Tiger Beer needed to prove that it could produce a quality product, one that is on par with what is produced in the West. And it seems that Tiger Beer has never relinquished its tight control over its product quality. I suppose having Heineken as a partner helped because Heineken is known to be extremely particular about quality and consistency.

But why did Fraser and Neave launch a new brand and not just license one?

Building a new brand from scratch is not an easy thing to do, even in 1932. The beer market was very competitive then and there were already many entrenched players in the market. Fraser and Neave could have just licensed the Heineken brand and brewed the beer in Singapore for distribution in Asia Pacific. That seemed like a better and easier move. After all, the marriage of the Heineken brand with Fraser and Neave's local market knowledge and distribution network would have been excellent. Trying to build a new brand out of nothing is tough. Any other company would probably have taken the easier route of leveraging on the Heineken brand name and its European heritage.

Fraser and Neave decided to launch a new brand because there was no other brand in the market at that time that was Asian in origin yet possessed all the qualities of a top-notch Western brewed beer. In this respect, Tiger Beer was pioneering a brand new category. It was not launching a new brand into an existing category called *Asian beer* that already had a very strong brand in it. At that time, this new category called *Asian beer* was empty and Tiger Beer could lead in this category. Powerful brands are built by creating new categories. If you look at some of the world's most successful brands in the world today, you will find that they each pioneered a new category.

In the beverage industry, there are many cases of successful brands being built on the back of new categories. Coca-Cola was not the first soft drink in the world but it pioneered a new category called *cola* and became the world's No. 1 soft drinks brand even in the face of aggressive challenger brands. Pepsi was late into the cola market but it pioneered a sub category within cola that made it a very strong No. 2, and that sub category is called *cola for young people*. Pepsi acknowledges that Coke is the real thing but being the real thing also makes it a very old brand. And Pepsi is the young thing that is specially designed for young people or those who are young at heart. Actually Pepsi is also a very old brand, almost as old as Coca-Cola! Dr Pepper pioneered a new category called *spicy cola* and became very successful. 7-Up pioneered a new category called *clear cola* and became very successful.

Even among beer brands, many of the successful ones were built on the back of a new category. When Heineken first launched in the United States, it was up against the toughest and most seasoned of competitors. Other than Budweiser, Miller and Coors, there were a host of other brands. But Heineken made a name for itself by pioneering a category called *premium import*. Samuel Adams pioneered a new category called *microbrewed beer*. Miller pioneered a new category called *light beer*. Asahi pioneered a new category called *Japanese beer*. Tsingtao pioneered a new category called *Chinese beer*. So, Tiger Beer was in good company. It pioneered a new category called *exotic Asian beer* that nobody had claimed at that time.

The way to build a strong brand is to own a category, and the best way to own a category is to create that category and then promote the category aggressively. You see, nobody is really interested in your brand. Whatever you say about your brand is biased because it is your brand. But if you have a new category and you promote that category, people are more likely to listen. People are interested in what is new. When you have a new category, promote that category. When you promote that category, you are seen as the leader, and when that category grows, your brand grows with it.

Tiger Beer has done the right thing by promoting the category and not the brand. In its key Western markets, Tiger Beer trades on its Asian heritage and not the brand itself. It promoted this new category called *exotic Asian beer* and all the mystique and romance that are associated with the Far East. When this category grew, Tiger Beer grew along with it. There are challenges, of course, and we will look at them in Chapter 6. By promoting the category, Tiger Beer grows the category and is seen as the category leader. When the category grows, Tiger Beer grows. It is always good to stake out your own turf as early as possible.

I also think that Fraser and Neave did the right thing by launching a new brand because brands can last forever and brands can influence buying decisions. Remember those blind taste tests for beer that show that when people do not know what they are drinking, the beers are rated quite similar in terms of the quality of taste? But when they know the brand they are drinking, the perceived differences in taste become more exaggerated. So, beer is a brand-sensitive category. The brand of the beer you drink tells the world who you are, what you are. Everything else being equal, what makes you buy what you buy? The brand, of course.

People drink a certain brand of beer because it says certain things about them. If you drink Tiger Beer, it says something about you. And that is why you drink Tiger Beer. Hence, the brand is a powerful strategic asset for any business, and Fraser and Neave made the right move by creating a brand that it could own. Building that brand was difficult but after all the hard work is done, the brand will take over the work of driving the growth of the business.

GROWING PAINS

IMITATION—THE HIGHEST FORM OF FLATTERY

Well, that is what they say. But if you have ever had your products ripped off by counterfeiters, you would not find that very flattering. For Tiger Beer, however, the situation was different in 1937. The Royal Air Force took inspiration from the Tiger Beer logo and made it part of their squadron's logo. Now, doesn't that show that Tiger Beer was an iconic brand even back then? The following excerpt, taken from the *Royal Air Force: History of No. 230 Squadron*, says it all:

In front of a palm tree eradicated, a tiger passant guardant—approved by HRH King George VI in February 1937. The badge commemorated the Squadron's association with Malaya, the traveller's palm being a reference to the long flights so often undertaken and the tiger is said to have been inspired by the labels on the bottles of the local Singaporean brew.

THE FAMINE YEARS

With the ravages of World War Two, Tiger Beer faced a severe shortage of raw materials, such as glass, and basic beer making ingredients, such as malt barley, hops and yeast. So, what did the folks at Tiger Beer do to survive?

Well, they brewed a lighter beer called Tiger Cub. It was an ingenious solution, considering the limited supply of raw materials. Now, Tiger Cub was not as strong in taste as the original brew but it was better than not having any beer at all. Tiger Cub beer was brewed and sold to the public until 1947 when it was retired to make way for the *real* Tiger Beer.

In January of 1947, to prepare for the return of the full-strength brew, APB—Tiger Beer's parent company— ran print advertisements in cartoon format. The first showed a tiger lifting weights, and was headlined by the simple and catchy "Tiger Cub. Gathering Strength." A follow-up print advertisement showed the Tiger Cub taking a bow on a stage, accompanied by these words:

> Ladies and Gentlemen: I thank you with all my gathered strength for your support during my year as understudy to 'TIGER'. In making my last bow, I know my part will be taken by a stronger and more mature performer. I wish you farewell and many a happy TIME FOR A TIGER.

With this print advertisement, Tiger Beer returned to the scene, much to the relief of not just Tiger Beer but beer drinkers in general. Nobody wants to drink a Tiger Beer that is not the full strength version. It is just not the same.

TIGER CUB
Gathering Strength

Ladies and Gentlemen:
I thank you with all my gathered strength,
for your support during my year
as understudy to "TIGER".
In making my last bow,
I know my part will be taken
by a stronger and more mature performer
I wish you farewell
and many a happy TIME FOR A TIGER

BEYOND LAGER BEER

Tiger Beer has been brewed exclusively in Asia since 1932 using malt barley imported from Australia and hops imported from Germany. The yeast used in the brewing of the beer is cultured exclusively for the brand in Holland. The combination of ingredients and Tiger Beer's brewing process create a distinctive taste that is clean, crisp and with a hint of a bitter aftertaste.

However, Tiger Beer was not content with just being a lager beer. It wanted to expand its product range. And so Tiger Beer added the Tiger Stout and Tiger Extra Stout to its range. But doing so meant line-extending the Tiger brand name into an area that it was not known for. Line extensions can cause confusion in the market.

Witness what happened to Budweiser and Miller. There were too many products carrying the Budweiser and Miller brand names, which got too confusing. In the long run, line extension can damage a brand. I believe that focus is the reason Heineken and Carlsberg became such strong brands. One brand, one beer. Of course, Heineken and Carlsberg had the advantage of being European in the first place but the principle works even if you are a beer from Singapore.

After the war, Malayan Breweries, which brewed Tiger Beer, merged with the Archipelago Brewery Company, which brewed

Anchor Beer and Diamond Lager Beer. The decision was taken to focus the brands. Tiger Beer would focus on lager and a new brand, ABC Stout, was created for the stout line. That was a smart move. It allowed Tiger Beer to focus on being the best lager beer from Asia, and ABC Stout could concentrate on the stout market. One brand, one beer. That is the way to grow.

THE HARD WORK PAID OFF

TIGER BEER—ONE OF SINGAPORE'S 15 MOST VALUABLE BRANDS

In 2002, International Enterprise Singapore (IE Singapore)— the government agency tasked with helping Singapore companies build a stronger presence in international markets—launched the Singapore Brand Award. This is an award given out to the 15 most valuable brands in Singapore. The Singapore Brand Award adopts the same methodology that BusinessWeek uses for its Top 100 Global Brands table. In 2002, APB was valued at S$820 million. In 2003, that value increased to S$943 million. In both years, APB was ranked fourth out of 15 companies.

In 2003, the Singapore Brand Award also included a Brand Strength Table that evaluates how strong a brand is in its key markets. Tiger Beer ranked joint third with the other tiger, Tiger Balm, with a score of 57 per cent. The top spot went to Singapore Airlines with a score of 60 per cent. This puts Tiger Beer as one of Singapore's best brands.

In 2004, APB's value increased to S$1.14 billion, making it the fourth most valuable brand in Singapore. In 2005, the value jumped again to S$1.23 billion, again the fourth most valuable brand in

Singapore. At the last ranking exercise in 2006, APB saw an 11 per cent increase in its value to S$1.36 billion, keeping it still in fourth spot overall. In that year, the most valuable Singapore brand was SingTel at S$2.67 billion.

There has not been any valuation done on the Tiger Beer brand itself and how much of APB's value was contributed by Tiger Beer is hard to say because the study was based only on publicly available financial data. But I think it must have been considerable since Tiger Beer is APB's flagship brand. Here is a chronological tour of Tiger Beer's illustrious career from 1932 till 2007.

MILESTONES IN TIGER BEER'S HISTORY	
1932	Malayan Breweries Limited brews the first batch of Tiger Beer on 1 October at its Alexandra Road brewery, which is today the Tiger Beer international headquarters.
1933	Sir Cecil Clementi, Governor of Singapore, takes a tour of the brewery and is satisfied with what he sees. By now, Tiger Beer is flying off the shelves and the company begins drawing up plans to export the brew.
1937	The Royal Air Force Squadron 230, based at Seletar in Singapore, likes Tiger Beer so much that it models its regimental insignia after the tiger and palm tree in the Tiger Beer logo. Thankfully, the pilots do not drink while they are flying.
1939	Only seven years old, Tiger Beer takes on beers from all over the Commonwealth in the prestigious Bottled Beer Competition and wins its first international beer medal, one of many medals that will soon follow.

1945	The shortage of malt barley, hops and glass caused by World War Two gives rise to a less strong but still rather tasty version of the beer, fittingly called Tiger Cub. Once production is restored after the war, Tiger Beer's appeal starts spreading to other countries as Allied servicemen who were stationed in Singapore took crates of their good old friend, the Tiger Beer, home with them. No surprises then that Tiger Beer is also known as a 'soldier's beer'.
1946	Anthony Burgess adopts Tiger Beer's slogan "Time For A Tiger" as the title of his new book, *Time for a Tiger*. The first part of his Malayan trilogy, *The Long Day Wanes*, is set in the twilight of British rule of the peninsula.
1954	Tiger Beer wins its first ever gold medal at the Commonwealth Bottled Beer Competition.
1965	In keeping with world trends, Tiger Beer launches its first canned beer.
1973	Tiger Beer makes its very first television commercial for the Singapore market.
1981	Tiger Beer makes its first appearance in the ultra competitive markets of the United Kingdom and Germany.
1990	Asia Pacific Breweries (the new name of Tiger Beer's parent company) migrates Tiger Beer production to a new, state-of-the art brewery at Tuas, Singapore. This new brewery was built at the cost of S$200 million.
1991	Tiger Beer enters the New Zealand market, a move which marks its first phase of regional expansion.

1993	Tiger Beer expands into Vietnam and China.
1998	Tiger Beer wins the World's Best Lager Beer award at the BIIA Competition in the United Kingdom.
2004	Tiger Beer wins the Gold Medal at the prestigious World Beer Cup.
2005	Jessica Alba becomes the first Hollywood actress to star in a Tiger Beer TV commercial.
2007	Tiger Beer is now sold in Papua New Guinea as it celebrates its 75th anniversary.

A 1930s file picture of a Tiger Beer promoter.

TIGER BEER

虎標啤酒

CHOP RIMAU

BIR YANG TERBAIK

2

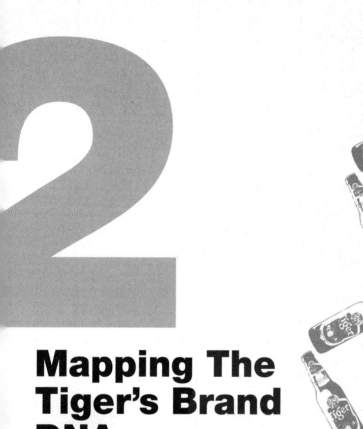

Mapping The Tiger's Brand DNA

In order for any brand to be successful, it must have a strong brand

DNA. The brand DNA simply refers to the things that make a brand what it is. A strong brand DNA will allow the brand to cut through all the clutter in the market. What is the sign of a strong brand DNA in any brand? If you take away the logo and the name, and people are still able to tell that it is your brand, then that is a strong brand DNA.

For example, part of the Coca-Cola DNA is the patented Coke bottle design and the fact that Coke is "The Real Thing". These are the elements that make Coca-Cola what it is. Take away the logo and the brand name, and you can still tell that it is Coca-Cola. Although Tiger Beer has not gotten to the stage where Coca-Cola is now, it has still done a great job of creating and developing the Tiger Beer brand DNA. In this chapter, we will look at the things that make a Tiger Beer … a Tiger Beer. These are the things that define the Tiger Beer brand. They are the strands that make up the Tiger Beer brand DNA.

THE BUILDING BLOCKS

THE CATEGORY—LAGER

Tiger Beer is a lager beer. There is no Tiger Beer Lite, Tiger Beer Ice, Tiger Beer Draft, Tiger Beer Strong Brew, Tiger Beer Pilsner or Tiger Beer Dark. Tiger Beer stands for lager and nothing else. It is closely identified with that category of being a lager beer. Category is what defines the brand, not the other way around. People are not interested in the brand. When you promote the brand, you have a vested interest and hence people are more wary. But when you promote the category, people are more interested especially if it is a new category.

Unfortunately for Tiger Beer, the lager category is not new. It is 500 years old. And so, the Tiger team had to create a new category for the brew. In the West, Tiger Beer is a cool beer because it is promoted as an exotic Asian lager beer. So, that is the new category that Tiger Beer is identified with. Tiger Beer equals exotic Asian lager beer.

It is a different story in Asia where being Asian is no big deal. An Asian American friend of mine once told me that she is just another Asian girl when she is in Asia but when she is in New York, she is perceived as exotic. It is the same thing that happened to Tiger Beer—two different perceptions that has forced a dual brand strategy on the company. That is why Tiger Beer is promoted differently in Asia.

For a brand to be successful, it must define very clearly the category that it is in. In the Western markets, Tiger Beer is the *exotic Asian beer* and the advertising tag line it uses is "Discover The Tiger". In Asia, however, Tiger Beer is positioned as the "World Acclaimed" Asian beer, one that has won over 40 international beer competition awards. Why? Because Singapore is not known as a beer brewing nation and hence, the beer needs validation from the West to be seen as a great beer. And the brand needs to be strongly identified with its category. It must be seen as the category leader. It must be seen as the brand that defines the category.

However, Tiger Beer has two different categories. Isn't that confusing? Wouldn't that have created chaos in the minds of Tiger Beer's customers? I would have thought so but Tiger Beer has played its cards very carefully to ensure consistency in how the brand is promoted in Asian markets and in the West. There is

IN 1977 THE ASIAN WALL STREET JOURNAL
VOTED US BEST BREW.

(THEY'VE ALWAYS HAD HIGH STANDARDS.)

World Acclaimed   Tiger

no overlap. The world is a very big place after all. People in the United Kingdom who drink Tiger Beer and see it as a premium Asian brand will not be too disappointed, I think, to find that in Asia, Tiger Beer is a mass market brand (especially in Singapore and Malaysia) priced below the likes of Heineken, Carlsberg and Beck's. Well, they might be a little bit surprised but I do not think that it would be too damaging to the brand. After all, Heineken in its home country is positioned as a mainstream everyday beer. In its export markets, Heineken is positioned as a premium brand. The important thing is that Tiger Beer is very clear in its market segmentation and very consistent in the way it promotes the brand in the various regions. No overlap. No switching of strategies back and forth. There is clear demarcation of which regions use what strategy and consistent communications.

Come to think of it, this is actually quite a clever way of getting around the biggest problem facing Tiger Beer. It is Asian in nature, and beer is predominantly a Western cultural import. Being an Asian beer is a disadvantage in both the West and the East. More than that, Tiger Beer is from Singapore, a country known more for its ban on the humble chewing gum than for brewing beer. As such, straddling two categories is necessary. But the common denominator is that Tiger Beer is a lager beer. This is important because if people cannot even identify what category your brand falls into, then it is unlikely they will buy your brand.

If you can break down the process that Tiger Beer's customers use to look at the beer, you will probably find this. In the West: "Tiger Beer is an exotic Asian lager beer that carries a premium price." In the East: "Tiger Beer is an award-winning Asian lager beer that is enjoyed by all around the world."

WHAT'S IN THE NAME?

The name is probably the single most important branding decision that you can make in the long run. Why? Because whatever unique selling proposition that can make you famous and successful in the short run will be gone in the longer term because competitors will copy what you do, and maybe they can do it better and sell it cheaper. That is simply the nature of business. Whatever you do will be copied by your competitors—if it happens to be a good idea.

An excellent example is Xerox. In 1959, Xerox was the first automatic plain paper photocopier and the only one. So, it was easy to sell a Xerox in 1959. Today, all photocopiers are the same but what differentiates Xerox from the rest is nothing more than the name, and it is a fantastic name.

In my view, a good brand name must adhere to ten basic rules. It must be short, unique, memorable, easy to pronounce and language neutral. It must work in the English language and be linked to a category name. It must have a dot.com suffix. It must not use acronyms. And finally, the name must not be a generic word.

Looking at the Tiger Beer brand name, I would say that it meets most of the rules of naming. The name is of the ideal length—two syllables but three syllables if you see it as 'Tiger Beer' and not 'Tiger'. Most of the best names in the world are two syllables long: Google, Xerox, Yahoo!, eBay, Kodak, Lexus, iPod, Apple, Pixar, Disney, MySpace, Facebook, YouTube, Hyflux, FedEx, DeWalt, Otis, Prada, Gucci, Chanel, and the list goes on and on. It does not mean that a one-syllable name is no good, but two syllables seem to be the ideal.

The name 'Tiger' is not a unique name because it is the name of an animal, but when it is used out of context—the way Mango is

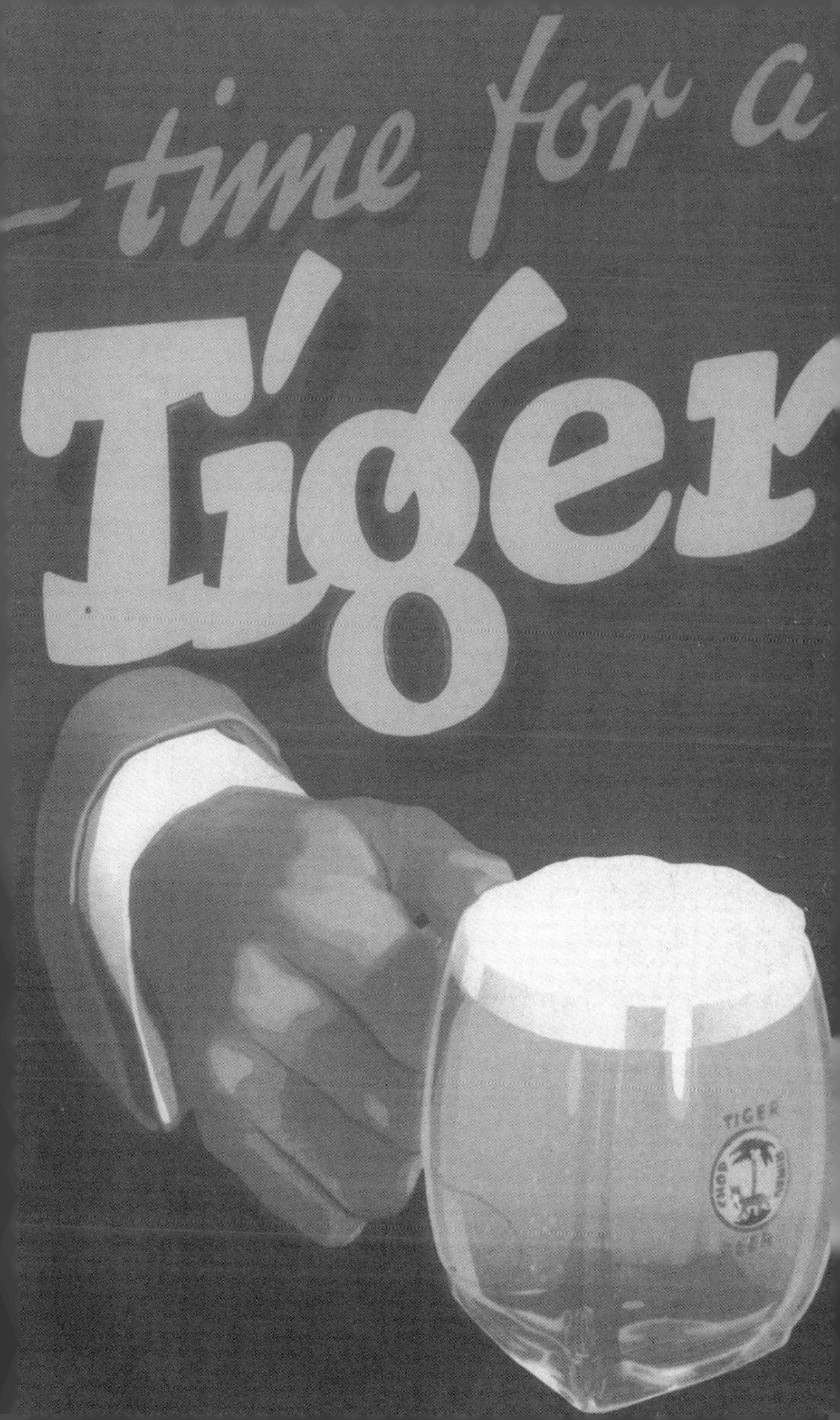

—time for a
Tiger
TIGER

used for a fashion brand, Orange is used for a telecommunications company and Mustang is used for a sports car—the name 'Tiger' is fine. Although 'Tiger' is a generic word, which violates one of the rules, in the world of beer, the name 'Tiger Beer' is unique only to this brand.

Indeed, it is quite a memorable name. The tiger being an Asian animal lends mystique to the beer. In a world where beers are given names like Heineken, Carlsberg, Beck's, Amstel, Budweiser, Miller and Tuborg, the name 'Tiger' certainly is quite special. It conjures up images of strength, authority and nobility. Now these are attributes that you want in a beer brand, or any brand for that matter.

'Tiger' is also very easy to pronounce and it works well in the English language. Even non-native speakers of the language would be able to pronounce it quite easily unless they are completely illiterate, but then you can't blame that on the brand.

Whether the name is language neutral, I am not so sure. Tiger Beer is currently sold in 60 countries and the name has not faced any violent objections in any of those places. So far, so good. This is important for an international beer like Tiger Beer because if the name means something bad in a foreign country where the beer is sold, the damage to the brand can be irreparable. The Ford Pinto did not sell well in Brazil because *pinto* in Brazilian Portuguese means 'small penis' and nobody wants to drive a car with a name like that! The Chevrolet Nova did not sell well in Spanish-speaking countries because *nova* in Spanish means 'no go'. I do not know about you but if I buy a car, I want it to go very fast, not stand still.

Tiger Beer might run into some problems with its name in the future as it expands, but it can cross the bridge when it gets there. Since tiger is the name of an animal, I think any bad associations with the name could be overcome as all cultures in the world know what a tiger is (the animal, that is). On the other hand, because the name generally connotes positive images, Tiger Beer faces another problem, which is that of other beverage companies trying to use the name. To date, these include an energy drink brand, a wine brand and some microbreweries.

Tiger Beer is also linked to a category (we discussed that earlier) and it has a dot.com suffix, which is increasingly important in this globalised world where a dot.com means that you do not have to register a separate website address for each country that you enter. A dot.com is a unifying suffix. And on the World Wide Web, a dot.com makes you look bigger than you are. A dot.com is a first class Netizen. A dot.com. [+ country suffix] is a second class Netizen. A dot.biz or dot.net are also not viewed as favourably as a dot.com suffix. It's not fair, I know, but that is the way it works. And Tiger Beer has its own dot.com suffix (www.tigerbeer.com).

In the world of brands, the name is very important and it is no different for beers. Beck's is a top German beer brand and Germany is a country that is famous for beer. But Beck's is a name that could sound German or British. To some, it might sound British; to others, German. To me, Heineken, which is Dutch, sounds more German than Beck's. I'm sure Beck's and Heineken will object to this view but that is the way I see it. 'Tiger Beer' sounds Asian but it does not tie the brand down to a single Asian country, which was exactly what Tiger Beer wanted. It makes Tiger Beer more mobile compared to beers like Tsingtao, which is very obviously Chinese in origin, and Asahi, which ties it to Japan. China and Japan are also not traditionally known as beer brewing countries so being too closely tied to their home country means that these brands are less mobile. Furthermore, because the tiger is an exclusively Asian animal, it creates the right brand association for Tiger Beer. Now, are you starting to see why the name 'Tiger' has been so important to the beer's success?

One more thing. Drinking beer is seen as a masculine activity. So, you want a name that sounds macho. What is more macho than a tiger? In fact, the name is so macho that Tiger Beer is trying hard to play down the macho element so that it does not look like it is trying too hard with the word play on the name. I think that is the right thing to do because if you try too hard to be macho, people will see you as insecure. Just like if you try too hard to be cool, then you become very uncool. Furthermore, Tiger Beer wants the beer to appeal to a broader audience including female drinkers who actually form quite a high percentage of the beer drinking population. So, trying to be overly macho may put off the female drinkers.

THE TASTE

The thing with beer is that, unlike wine, beer tastes best when it is fresh. So, Tiger Beer tries hard to brew its beer as close to its key markets as possible to maintain its freshness. Although most beer brewers will tell you that beer is best consumed within six months of the brewing date, in my experience, anything over a month starts to deteriorate rapidly. I've also noticed that not many brewers stamp the brew date on the can the way Tiger Beer does.

Every time I buy a Tiger Beer, I look at the can to see the brew date. Most of the cans I see are less than three weeks old. That is the advantage of having a brewery so close to home. Asia Pacific Breweries (APB) has some 30 breweries in 12 countries as of August 2007. Tiger Beer is brewed in ten of these countries. This is a powerful advantage for the brand. The people at Tiger Beer could say: "Tiger Beer is brewed at a brewery close to you so that it tastes fresher than the imports." Of course, this can only work in markets that Tiger Beer has a brewery but it is worth a shot.

Tiger Beer also works very hard to ensure the consistency of the taste from country to country and from batch to batch. In this respect, I think Tiger Beer has done a better job than Coca-Cola. Coca-Cola may be the most valuable brand in the world but it is far from being consistent in terms of taste as there seems to be variations in taste among countries. How does Tiger Beer maintain consistency in taste despite it being sold in so many countries? Once a month, every brewery is required to send samples to Heineken in The Netherlands for taste testing. Each brewery also has a brewmaster who tests the beer on a daily basis. These procedures certainly keep the breweries on their toes! And every month, Tiger Beer gives out a Tiger Quality Award to the brewery that maintains the best taste consistency. Tiger Beer is very consistent and it is that consistency that has built confidence in the brand. Consistency is a characteristic of a brand that knows what is important to its customers.

I'm not a beer expert but compared to imported beers from Europe, Tiger Beer tastes slightly more bitter and more yeasty than the European imports, which are sweeter. I believe that the taste of Tiger Beer must support the masculine image that the name projects. A brand is also about promise and delivery. When you have a name like 'Tiger Beer', it promises something that is strong, and the taste had better deliver on that promise. Whether you like it or not, your brand makes a promise and that promise has to be delivered in order for the brand to grow strong. In this case, Tiger Beer delivered on the taste. And judging by the number of awards that Tiger Beer has won, I'm not the only one who thinks so.

DRESSING IT UP

THE LOGO

A brand is more than just a logo although branding did start out as a logo some 4,000 years ago. In those days cattle owners had difficulty telling each other's cows apart and so they branded their stock with a branding iron that carried their initials or logo.

Tiger Beer was first brewed in 1932 but the current logo with the shield and the unique 'Tiger' typeface was created only 30 years later in 1962. What you see on the Tiger Beer bottle these days is a refinement of the logo that was first established in 1962. What is so special about the Tiger Beer logo? Well, to answer that, I will have to tell you the fascinating story of how the logo evolved.

The Tiger Beer logo is based on the tiger, an animal that is immediately recognised as an Asian animal. Many legends and myths surround this proud and magnificent creature, which lend some sense of origin, heritage and mystique to the brand. The tiger also symbolises strength, power, agility and confidence—the kind of positive attributes that Tiger Beer (or any other brand for that matter) would like to be associated with.

But even with all these, Tiger Beer has imposed some very strict guidelines on how the animal is represented in the logo. For a start, it does not want the animal to look too much like a real tiger as it feels

that would make the brand overly aggressive. Still, the animal is realistic enough that people will know it is a tiger.

In the logo, the tiger always faces left and always stands under a palm tree, which interestingly enough, was originally a coconut tree. In those days, tigers were commonly seen roaming around coconut trees. Over time, the coconut tree evolved into a palm tree.

Look carefully and you will see that the tiger is enclosed within a circle. The purpose for this is to keep it symbolically 'caged'. By caging the tiger, Tiger Beer has more control over how it is portrayed because if it is allowed out of the cage, then it can potentially be made to do a lot of things, like jump, stretch and pounce. Tiger Beer is concerned that there would be the temptation to exercise too much creativity which may lead to questionable brand identity, comical communication executions and confusion with other tiger logos in the market. Caging the tiger means that there will not be too much variation in the look. So, the tiger is always caged. In 1993, however, to signify Tiger Beer's rapid growth in the region, the tiger was allowed to put one paw slightly out of the circle.

Also, the way the letters are represented in the word 'Tiger' is unique to the brand, with its hidden symbolic elements. The letter 'i' 'looks like the numeral '1', which is something that every brand desires—to be No. 1 in its category. Bet you never noticed that. The letter 'g' is purposely designed to look like the numeral '8'. This is an auspicious number to the Chinese because '8', when pronounced in Mandarin and Cantonese, sounds like the word for 'prosperity'. Plus, it looks rather stylish. The 'e' is adopted from the Heineken typeface to link Tiger Beer back to one of its parents. The folks at Tiger Beer commonly refer to that 'e' as the smiling 'e'.

The three colours of the Tiger Beer logo—blue, amber and gold—are also significant. The blue represents pure water. (Water is a major ingredient in beer and the quality of the water has an impact on the taste of the beer.) Amber is the colour of the brew and subtly ties the logo back to the product it represents. Finally, gold represents Tiger Beer's winning ways as well as links the brand back to the gold medals that it has won over the decades.

Just like any progressive brand, the Tiger brand has had its logo gradually altered over time to keep it looking fresh and up to date. But always, the changes were carefully considered so as not to damage the brand's identity. If you look at the different logos from 1932 till now, you can still tell that the current logo is descended from the original. In this respect, Tiger Beer has done very well to maintain a consistent look and feel for its brand.

The original 1932 Tiger Beer logo (above left) and the logo today.

Complementing the logo, of course, is the bottle, which has always been glass and amber in colour. The dark colour serves two purposes: it identifies the brand and also protects the beer from damage that can be caused by the sun's ultraviolet rays. The brew is also served in a blue aluminium can but where glass bottles are used, it is always the same amber glass bottle. That bottle is part of the Tiger Beer DNA as much as the taste and the logo.

The original beer can of 1965 and quart bottle of 1932.

THE AWARDS AND ACCOLADES

Tiger Beer has won over 40 international beer awards. This is part of the Tiger Beer heritage. This is part of the brand's DNA—an award winning beer. Here is a quick look at all the international acclaims that Tiger Beer has won in its 75 years of brewing quality beer.

1939 Bronze medal at the Bottled Beer Competition, organised by the Brewing Trade Review (British Empire Overseas), London. This was Tiger Beer's first ever award and marked the beginning of its journey as a champion beer brand.

1946 Anthony Burgess used Tiger's advertising slogan, "Time For A Tiger", as the title of his book.

1954 Overall Gold (Championship) at The Bottled Beer Competition at The Brewers' Exhibition, organised by The Trades, Markets & Exhibitions Ltd, London.

1964 Silver (First Place) at the Commonwealth Bottled Beer Competition held by The Brewing, Bottling & Allied Trades Exhibition in London.

1968 Gold Medal at the 7th Selection Mondiale, held by the Institut Pour Les Selction De La Qualite in Germany.

1970 Gold Medal (Championship) at the Commonwealth Bottled Beer Competition held by The Brewing, Bottling & Allied Trades Exhibition in London.

1971 Overall Gold Medal and Diploma For Excellence at the Lager Beer Competition, organised by the British Bottlers Institute.

1977 Best Brew title at the International Beer Contest held in Hong Kong by the *Asian Wall Street Journal*.

1978 Overall Gold Medal at the 17th Selection Mondiale, held by the Institut Pour Les Selection De La Qualite in Geneva.

1979 Overall Gold Medal at the 18th Selection Mondiale, held by the Institut Pour Les Selection De La Qualite in Paris.

1980 Overall Gold Medal at the 19th Selection Mondiale, held by the Institut Pour Les Selection De La Qualite In Vienna.

1980 "Top Taste of Lager" award at the International Blind Tasting of Beers by *The Sunday Times* in London.

1982 Overall Gold Medal at the 21st Selection Mondiale, held by the Institut Pour Les Selection De La Qualite in London.

1982 Diploma of Excellence (Class E) at the Lager Beer Competition, held by the British Bottlers Institute.

1983 Overall Gold Medal at the 22nd Selection Mondiale, held by the Institut Pour Les Selection De La Qualite in Rome.

1983 Diploma of Excellence (Class D) at the Lager Beer Competition, held by the British Bottlers Institute.

1984 Gold Medal (Brewing Excellence) and Gold Medal (Superior Taste & Quality) at the International Monde Cup Competition, held by the Institut Pour Les Selection De La Qualite.

1984 Gold Medal at the 23rd Selection Mondiale, held by the Institut Pour Les Selection De La Qualite in Madrid.

1985 Gold Medal (Can & Bottle) at the 24th Selection Mondiale, held by the Institut Pour Les Selection De La Qualite in London.

1986 Overall Gold (International Quality Display) at the 25th Selection Mondiale, held by the Institut Pour Les Selection De La Qualite in Geneva.

1986 Silver Medal at the Lager Beer Competition, held by the British Bottlers Institute.

1987 Gold Medal (Can & Bottle) at the 26th Selection Mondiale, held by the Institut Pour Les Selection De La Qualite in Brussels.

1988 Gold Medal at the 27th Selection Mondiale, held by the Institut Pour Les Selection De La Qualite in Athens.

1988 Voted as "Positively The Best Beer In The World" by *The Washingtonian*.

1990 Gold Medal at the 29th Selection Mondiale, held by the Institut Pour Les Selection De La Qualite in Luxemborg.

1991 Grand Gold at the 30th Selection Mondiale, held by the Institut Pour Les Selection De La Qualite in Barcelona. This is the first time that it has won the Grand Gold.

1992 Gold Medal (Can & Bottle) at the 31st Selection Mondiale, held by the Institut Pour Les Selection De La Qualite in Amsterdam.

1993 Gold Medal (Can & Bottle) at the 32nd Selection Mondiale, held by the Institut Pour Les Selection De La Qualite in Brussels.

1994 Tiger Beer brewery in Tuas, Singapore, was conferred the ISO9002 certificate by Lloyd's of London for quality management systems.

1995 Silver Medal at the Australian International Beer Awards, organised by the Royal Agricultural Society of Victoria and the University of Ballarat.

1995 Gold Medal at the 34th Selection Mondiale, held by the Institut Pour Les Selection De La Qualite in Rome.

1996 Tiger Beer was rated as one of the world's Top 10 Beers in "The World's Greatest Brands" published by Interbrand.

1996 Silver Medal at the Australian International Beer Awards, organised by the Royal Agricultural Society of Victoria and the University of Ballarat.

1996 Silver Medal at the Selection Mondiale, held by the Institut Pour Les Selection De La Qualite in Rome.

1997 Silver Medals (Pint & Can categories) at the Australian International Beer Awards, organised by the Royal Agricultural Society of Victoria and the University of Ballarat.

1998 Gold Medal (Class 2 Lager Category) for bottled and canned lager, and overall Gold Championship Medal at the Brewing Industry International Awards, Brewing Technology Services in London.

2001 *FHM* voted Tiger Beer as a 5-star beer and the top brew in Australia and United Kingdom.

2004 Gold Medal (European Style Pilsner) at the 2004 World Beer Cup organised by The Association of Brewers.

2004 Recognised as a CoolBrandLeader at the UK CoolBrand Leaders competition organised by the Superbrands Council.

2005 Silver Medal (Premium Lager) in the Wine & Spirit International Beer Challenge.

2005 Recognised as a CoolBrandLeader at the UK CoolBrand Leaders competition organised by the Superbrands Council.

2005 Jumped from 14th to the 9th spot in the Brand Channel Readers' Choice Ranking 2005.

2006 Recognised as a CoolBrand Leader at the UK CoolBrand Leaders competition organised by the Superbrands Council.

Well, that is an extremely long and impressive list of awards that the relatively young Tiger Beer brand has won. Being an award-winning brand is part of the Tiger Beer DNA and the brand continues to strive for bigger awards. It needs that constant validation from the opinion leaders in the beer world to assure its customers (especially in Asia) that what they are drinking is at least as good as the imports from Europe, if not better. This is captured in Tiger Beer's new slogan, "World Acclaimed".

THE PACKAGING

Tiger Beer's packaging plays a crucial role in building its brand. A brand is not just about packaging; however, packaging is very important because people can see and touch the bottle and the can. And the packaging must help to differentiate the brand. Tiger Beer has always been served in an amber glass bottle. That colour differentiated the brand from Heineken, Carlsberg, Tuborg, Beck's and others, which are typically green. So far so good.

But Tiger Beer eventually had to introduce aluminium cans. While other beer brands like Heineken continued with the green theme for their cans, Tiger Beer decided not to use amber because amber looks dull and uninviting on aluminium. The name 'Tiger' says it is an energetic brand, so Tiger Beer chose an electric blue that immediately sets it apart from other beer brands on the shelves. It gives Tiger Beer a distinctive look and feel. You can easily tell which six-pack is a Tiger Beer from a distance just by its colour.

Tiger Beer's packaging forms one of the strands that make up its brand DNA, and Tiger Beer has maintained the consistency of its packaging design in all of its markets so that a Tiger is a Tiger is a Tiger regardless of which country you buy it from.

SUPPORTING THE BRAND

TIGER BEER'S FIVE BRAND PILLARS

At the centre of everything that Tiger Beer does is the strategic ambition of being seen as: "Asia's World Beer Since 1932. Distinctively Asia, Unmistakably World Class." To achieve this goal, Tiger Beer has developed five brand pillars that will support the brand in all aspects of brand development and communications. The brand pillars are Authority, Innovation, Emotive Image, Touch Points and Connection Platform.

AUTHORITY

The Authority pillar gives customers rational reasons to buy Tiger Beer. It is put in place to give Tiger Beer the external validation that it needs to survive in the global market. Tiger Beer is acutely aware that it comes from a country that does not have a heritage in beer brewing unlike Germany, which invented lager beer and has been brewing beer for over 500 years. So, if you are a lager beer from Germany, you will be seen as the real thing. No external validation is ever needed. But Tiger Beer is from Singapore and so external validation is a must for this brand. That is why Tiger Beer actively participates in beer competitions all over the world to win gold medals. It has to show that its beer is as good as anything from Europe, if not better. It helps that most of these competitions are held in Europe and winning there enhances Tiger Beer's credentials.

The Authority pillar also tries to further enhance the brand's image by carefully controlling where Tiger Beer is sold because where it is sold has some impact on the type of customers that the brand attracts. And the kind of people who drink your beer says a lot about your brand, just like the brand says a lot of the people who use it. All these things contribute to Tiger Beer's reputation.

INNOVATION

As Peter Drucker, the father of modern business management, once said: "A business has only two basic functions—innovation and marketing. Innovation and marketing produce results. The rest are just costs." I think Peter Drucker is right.

Tiger Beer is well known for its aggressive marketing but at the same time, it also focuses on innovation to keep ahead of the game. It needs to come up with new and exciting innovations to keep the brand fresh. Among their innovations is Tiger Crystal, which comes in an eye-catching flint bottle with pressure-sensitive clear plastic labels. Although Tiger Beer is a highly focused brand that stands for lager beer, the Tiger Crystal was introduced specially for China because Chinese beer drinkers find the taste of original Tiger Beer too full flavoured for their liking.

Another innovation that Tiger Beer adopted early on is the Super Cold, which is a method of serving colder and fresher beers. And then there are the unseen innovations such as constant improvements in the brewing process through the use of new technology and other such things. Tiger Beer also researches new global trends to see what would be considered 'cool' in the future. One result of this is the creation of a stunning shrink wrap label that envelopes their bottles.

EMOTIVE IMAGE

The Emotive Image pillar serves to provide consumers with an intangible reason to buy Tiger Beer. Its goal is to make Tiger Beer "cool enough to wear". Now, this is a difficult thing to achieve. It requires an inside out approach. You need to be cool inside before you can project a cool image to the outside world.

To achieve this, Tiger Beer must be associated with cool events, cool people and cool places, like hip bars and pubs. Tiger Beer seems to be doing quite all right in this department judging by the fact that it has been recognised as a CoolBrand Leader for three years running from 2004 to 2006 at the UK CoolBrand Leaders competition organised by the Superbrands Council. Besides being cool from the inside out, you also need other people to say that you are cool. The emotive image is an important part of the brand building process for Tiger Beer because people always buy on emotion but will defend that purchase on rational reasons.

TOUCH POINTS

The Touch Points pillar refers to how the brand interacts with its customers through its packaging design, point-of-sale displays, Tiger Beer merchandise, vehicle livery, uniforms and apparel. All these things are important touch points because they communicate the brand 24/7. Not only that, they have been carefully designed to communicate the brand in a consistent manner at all times so that customers are reassured.

CONNECTION PLATFORMS

The Connection Platforms pillar aims to bring the consumer in direct contact with the brand through events that are cool and trendy, such as the Tiger Translate events and the Tiger FC club. More about these is covered in Chapter 4. This pillar is aimed at creating a bond between the drinker and the brand via a unique and motivating experience. The connection platforms are relatively new, having been implemented only a few years ago, but Tiger Beer has struck a formula that is workable and scalable, and they are doing wonders for Tiger Beer's reputation. Tiger Beer intends to continue its efforts to create more such platforms, and will also enhance the existing platforms and propagate them in as many countries as it can.

Giving The Brand Its Wings

Tiger Beer began life as a mass-market beer

in its key markets of Singapore and Malaysia. That was my first impression of Tiger Beer, too. Its reputation of being a mass-market beer is strong since it is widely served in hawker centres around Singapore. Over time, however, Tiger Beer slowly shifted this mass-market position to a more upmarket one in these key places, but even then it is hard to change what is ingrained so deeply in the mind. As such, when Tiger Beer began to export the brand overseas, it had to decide whether to stick with its mass-market positioning or try something else.

In Singapore, Tiger Beer can be seen as being enjoyed at both the hawker centres and in hip pubs and clubs, perhaps because the beer is indigenous to Singapore. So, it is all right to be everywhere and everything to everyone since it got here first. There is some validity in this because if you get to the market first and grow bigger than everyone else, then you can stretch the brand a little bit more. But Tiger Beer decided to move away from the mass-market position when entering the international arena for several reasons—entrenched competition, high distribution costs and heritage.

THE FIRST HURDLES

ENTRENCHED COMPETITION

Beer is a highly competitive industry, and Tiger Beer would be faced with a lot of entrenched competition in many of those overseas markets where some of the players are far larger than Tiger Beer. Because of that, Tiger Beer had to employ the principle of force in dealing with these new markets. The principle of force is a military principle that states that the one with the larger army will have an advantage over the smaller army. But the smaller army can still win if it chooses its battles carefully, concentrating all its forces on one area and attacking that area vigorously.

Therefore, Tiger Beer chose to focus on being a specialist beer brand rather than trying to appeal to everyone because it knew it did not have the resources to fight on all fronts. Being a specialist brand allowed Tiger Beer to focus on carving out a niche for itself such as being *the* exotic, premium beer from the Far East. Being a niche player also allowed Tiger Beer to price itself higher than other brands.

DISTRIBUTION COSTS

Tiger Beer can compete on price in its home market of Singapore because it has a brewery there. Today, it has breweries in 12 countries but these are still Asian countries. There is no brewery in Europe or the United States, which means that Tiger Beer's distribution costs will be higher since the beer has to travel a longer distance. That higher cost factor meant it was difficult for Tiger Beer to be a mass-market player. They had to go premium by hook or by crook.

This is the same strategy that Heineken took when it ventured into the United States, one of the largest beer drinking markets in the world. In The Netherlands, Heineken is positioned as an everyday beer. But when it went to the United States, it had to be a premium imported beer because it could not compete with Budweiser and Miller on cost. So, Tiger Beer is in good company. And Tiger Beer's premium strategy in the United Kingdom and the United States seems to be working just fine.

HERITAGE

Tiger Beer lacks the heritage of the European brands, and a beer from Singapore has very little credibility. Therefore, Tiger Beer has had no choice but to narrow its focus to a group of people whom marketing folks call 'innovators'. Innovators are people who are game to try new things. They are adventurous and do not mind paying more for something new that they think is interesting or exciting. Tiger Beer used to be a trading brand served only in ethnic Chinese restaurants in the West but it has re-positioned itself to target this group of people in its key Western markets.

Where the Asian markets are concerned, Tiger Beer uses its long list of awards as a spearhead to give it credibility. If the beer is accepted by Western beer experts as a top beer, then it will be good enough for most Asian markets. The home market of Singapore, however, is more difficult to influence because people there are highly educated and more exposed to Western culture and Western brands. It will be an uphill struggle to change the mindsets there. Still, Tiger Beer is making good progress judging by the professionals who are now drinking Tiger Beer and think that the brew is cool.

Tiger Beer's medal icons. From left: the World Beer Cup, the British Bottlers Institute, and the Brewing Industry International Award.

London
was the setting for our first ever International Awards show in 1939.
We weren't expecting more than a postcard.

What we got, as well as a pleasant surprise, was our first international award, only seven years after our creation. However, after the stir we had created died down, we were proud to look back on an achievement that no other international beer brand could claim, so early in its history.

Given all the three factors—entrenched competition, distribution costs and heritage—Tiger Beer had no choice but to move away from its mass-market position and try to find a niche that it can occupy. Its venture overseas began in 1990 and took place in three phases—the first between 1990 and 1997, the second between 1998 and 2000, and the third from 2001.

Tiger Beer was exported to other countries prior to 1990 but a concerted effort was made only from that year onwards. Why? Well, Tiger Beer believed it needed to build up strength in its home market—considered to be Singapore and Malaysia due to the proximity and historical ties between these two countries—before venturing out.

THE TAKE-OFF

THE FIRST PHASE, 1990–1997

In the first phase of regionalisation, Asia Pacific Breweries (APB) expanded aggressively and established 16 breweries in nine countries so as to serve its target markets better. Having a brewery closer to its target market means that the beer can be fresher. Since beer deteriorates over time, having a brewery in a market that can churn out fresher beer can be the source of an unfair competitive advantage.

Furthermore, by having a brewery in the market itself, Tiger Beer also enjoys lower distribution, transportation and warehousing costs over time. There are also tax incentives that come from being locally situated. Being located in that market also sends out the signal that the market is important enough for Tiger Beer to invest in. It signals Tiger Beer's commitment to the market and creates a feel good factor. At S$1 billion, the initial investment for Phase One was not cheap but it represented an investment in Tiger Beer's future. It also showed that Tiger Beer was mature enough and confident enough to spread its footprint in the regional markets. However, this rapid regionalisation came with a lot of risk.

From a branding point of view, the biggest risk in any expansion is losing control of the brand in terms of its quality and consistency. Inconsistency can be very damaging to a brand, especially a young brand like Tiger Beer that is just venturing out of its comfort zone. Tiger Beer has had to work very hard on systems, processes and procedures. It also had to ensure that each country adheres to Tiger Beer's strict quality controls. In this respect, Tiger Beer's partnership with Heineken probably paid off in spades. Heineken is a stickler for quality. It is very relentless in testing for consistency amongst its many breweries and this has obviously rubbed off on Tiger Beer. Tiger Beer's fastidiousness with ensuring consistency and quality has helped the fledgling brand stamp its quality mark in its export markets.

THE SECOND PHASE, 1998–2000

Any brand that is spreading its wings will sometimes get caught up in the expansion frenzy and overstretch itself. It happens to most companies and it looked like APB would go that way. But the good thing is that it realised it had to consolidate its operations before all that expansion got out of hand. Between 1998 and 2000, APB did just that and consolidated its operations.

First, it streamlined its China operations by divesting the non-strategic Fuzhou Brewery. And then it divested its non-core businesses in New Zealand and Papua New Guinea, where it had expanded into the liquor and wine, and soft drinks businesses respectively. APB decided that it needed to stay focused on beer only or the brand will be distracted and damaged over time. That was a smart move!

Just as a plant needs to be constantly pruned in order to grow strong, so too do businesses and brands. Every now and then, brands need to prune their non-strategic assets and get rid of non-core or non-performing businesses to stay healthy.

THE THIRD PHASE, 2001 ONWARDS

After APB completed its consolidation and refocused its brand on the core business, it was ready to start growing again. The third phase of its expansion began with the construction of a new brewery in Hatay in Vietnam, and the doubling of the capacity of its brewery in Thailand. Both of these projects were completed by 2003.

APB also wanted to increase its presence in the Asia Pacific region with carefully selected acquisitions and green field breweries in countries like Sri Lanka, China, Mongolia and India. The expansion continued steadily. In 1992, APB had five breweries in three countries. In 2007, that number expanded to some 30 breweries in 12 countries. That is an impressive growth rate by any standards.

4

It's Not A Brand Until It's Famous

A Brand is not a brand until it's famous, and the way to make a brand famous is by communicating the brand clearly and consistently at all customer touch points at all times. But first, the brand message must be right. What is said is more important than how it is said. This is something that a lot of brands get wrong.

What about Tiger Beer? Has the brand figured out what to say before saying it? For the most part, yes. There have been some missteps along the way, of course, as with any brand that you care to mention, but mostly Tiger Beer has gotten the what-to-say part right. The how-to-say part was generally all right with the exception of a few misfires that happened along the way. We will examine those in the later part of this chapter.

TIGER BEER'S COMMUNICATIONS CHANNELS

Basically, brands are built with public relations but once the brand is built, it needs advertising to survive. Advertising is for maintenance. However, there are two product categories—cigarettes and beer— that are built and maintained by advertising because it is generally tough for these two products to get media publicity. It is easy to understand why this is so for cigarettes. Smoking is bad for health and sucking smoke into your lungs can't be good no matter how much of a cigarette fan you are. That is the reason why even smokers get very upset when they are forced to breathe in second-hand smoke. That is why cigarette brands require advertising to build.

Compared to cigarettes, beer is not that bad. Beer offers some health benefits (provided of course that you drink it in moderation) since it is made from malt barley and hops, and the alcohol content is relatively low, usually 5 per cent or thereabouts. But it is hard to get the media to write about beer. Beer is beer. It has been around for 2,000 plus years. What is there to write about? The media may occasionally write about wine as there are many different ways of making wine or so it seems, and wine is seen to be the drink of the sophisticated and upwardly mobile. But nobody writes about beer. One of the reasons could be that beer and beer making has not changed much over the centuries. Because it is still basically the same as it was, beer is a category that depends on advertising to build.

Tiger Beer was fortunate to receive rather generous publicity in the local daily, *The Straits Times*, when it was first launched in 1932. That was because Tiger Beer is Singapore's first lager beer and it was the first to be brewed in partnership with a leading European brewer. That publicity, however, was short-lived. Tiger Beer had to use advertising to build its brand, and I must say that over the decades, it has managed to create some memorable television commercials. In addition, Tiger Beer has also found some ingenious ways to generate millions of dollars' worth of publicity in the press recently. I will talk about this later. Right now, let us take a look at Tiger Beer advertising.

THE MESSAGES IN TIGER BEER'S ADVERTISING

Tiger Beer acknowledges that its advertising has played a big part in its success. Some of its campaigns have aged better than others but all of them have played their part in raising the Tiger Beer profile and helping Tiger Beer achieve certain marketing objectives.

Different approaches have worked in different markets. Tiger Beer discovered that Western glamour has proved to be popular in Asia, and so its Asian market advertisements are aimed at projecting Tiger Beer as part of the glamorous Western lifestyle that many Asians aspire to enjoy. Tiger Beer has done its market research well. It knows what to say to its Asian consumers.

Conversely, the Asian mystique has worked wonders in the West. In the words of one Tiger Beer Brand Champion (yes, that is what they call themselves on their name cards!), in Asia, it is no big deal being Asian. But in the West, being Asian has plenty of allure. With this knowledge on hand, Tiger Beer also knew what to say to its Western customers in its advertisements. In fact, its innovative advertisements that trade heavily on the brew's authentic Asian roots are attracting new Tiger Beer fans who are drawn by the Asian mystique that the brand has built up around it. It seems to be working. Tiger Beer is served in many of the hippest and most happening cities in the world. London. New York. Berlin. Boston. Moscow. Miami. You name a hip city and you are likely to find Tiger Beer being served in exclusive bars and pubs there. In the United Kingdom alone, Tiger Beer is served in over 8,000 pubs and clubs. Now, that is really something!

THE GENEALOGY

Tiger Beer has been running advertising campaigns on television for many years but the campaigns have not remained static. The table on page 76 gives you an overview of Tiger Beer's television commercials over the years.

Up till the year 2000, Tiger Beer advertising has been quite consistent in its direction and message as it was driven by Tiger Beer headquarters. The core idea it tried to impart was this: Tiger

Beer is a beer for winners. That is why you see consistent use of the tag lines "Good As Gold Around The World" and "Good As Gold", often accompanied by the voice-over: "Tiger Beer, winning the world over."

After 2000, with new people at the helm, this central control was relinquished and key local markets were given the leeway to develop their own campaigns. The reason for this shift was to give the brand a greater local flavour. And so, local faces were deemed right for Singapore; the Asian spirit (inward looking) was seen appropriate for Vietnam; and the challenger attitude seen to be fitting for Malaysia. These differences accounted for the many different styles of advertising.

The new direction, however, ignored the fact that Tiger Beer as a brand had by then built up some brand equity through its successful advertising campaigns over the previous years. Not continuing with the "Winning" theme created confusion and undid the good work. In 2006, however, Tiger Beer decided that central control was crucial to project a coherent brand image and maintain the brand's consistency. Let us now look at some of the more memorable Tiger Beer television campaigns from all eras.

EARTHQUAKE — THE FIRST TV COMMERCIAL (1973)

Made for the Singapore market, Tiger Beer's first ever TV commercial shows a group of men in a coffee shop drinking Tiger Beer. An earthquake erupts and the building begins to shake. While people panic and scramble for the exit, the men merely look around coolly and go back to drinking their beer. This commercial was designed to show that Tiger Beer is an unshakable beer and by extension, Tiger Beer drinkers too.

The commercial played the macho card. Macho works. Well,

TIGER BEER'S TELEVISION CAMPAIGNS				
	Regional positioning	Regional TV commercials (emotive advertising)	Regional TV commercials (rational advertising)	Local TV commercials (emotive advertising)
Pre 80s and 1980s	BEER FOR WINNERS	• Earthquake • Mark of a Winner I and II • Around The World • Others		
Late 80s to early 90s	REWARD FOR WINNERS	• Sailing • Romance • Underwater • Bobsled • Air Race • Others	• Local Boy Made Good • Cognoscenti	
Mid 90s	REWARD FOR WINNERS (who have performed a notable deed)	• Marlin • Sky Rescue • Matador	• Hallmark I	
End 90s to mid 2000			• Hallmark II • BIIA	Singapore: • High Adventure • What Time Is It? • Batman (Tiger Nation) • Star (Jessica Alba) Malaysia: • Genesis • Euphoria Vietnam: • Manifesto • One With The Lads • The Quest • Spill • Dance • Parade • Others
2006 onwards	WINNING	• Unravel the Secret (Tiger Ten)	• Unravel the Secret (Tiger Ten)	

in those days, beer was still a man's drink—and men like to be seen as unshakable. Of course, if that had been a real earthquake, nobody will think of you as unshakable if you had stayed in that coffee shop to finish up your beer. They will think of you as having a death wish! People know it is make believe. The most important thing is that the message got through—Tiger Beer drinkers are as unshakable as Tiger Beer itself.

AROUND THE WORLD (1978)

Within five short years, Tiger Beer television advertising changed tremendously. This commercial showed Tiger Beer being enjoyed around the world by successful, upwardly mobile people. It was meant to convey the message that Tiger Beer was no longer a local beer, that it had made its mark around the world, and that successful people—regardless of nationality—drink Tiger Beer. This was the first time that Tiger Beer made a concerted effort to project the brew as more than just a local brand. Tiger Beer's traditional stronghold was in Singapore, Malaysia and Vietnam but now that it was increasingly being exported to other countries, it needed a more international image.

REWARD FOR WINNERS CAMPAIGN (1988)

Ten years on, Tiger Beer advertising became even more sophisticated. The Underwater commercial—one of several in the Reward For Winners campaign—showed attractive people enjoying a lifestyle of the rich and famous on board a luxury yacht out in the open sea, getting a sun tan on the deck and, of course, enjoying an ice cold Tiger Beer. Tiger Beer wanted to position the brand as *the* beer for winners.

GOOD AS GOLD AROUND THE WO

Screen grab from the Underwater television commercial, part of the Reward For Winners campaign. Aired in Singapore, Vietnam and Cambodia in 1993 and 1995.

By then, it had won enough international awards to be confident enough to position the brand as "The Reward For Winners". Other than images of people on luxury yachts, the campaign also showed young and active people enjoying activities such as flying aeroplanes and bobsledding. The commercials end with this very famous Tiger Beer slogan: "Tiger. Good As Gold Around The World."

HALLMARK I (1996)

This commercial used plenty of gold imagery. It shows the Tiger brew flowing out of a bottle and then morph into a gold bar which carries the Tiger Beer logo and the numerals 999.99 (the numbers indicate the quality of the gold). The gold bar then begins to melt, only to pour into a beer glass and become Tiger Beer once again.

The commercial was meant to showcase Tiger Beer's Gold Medal achievements in international beer competitions. It continues the "Good As Gold" theme that was started by the Reward For Winners campaign. Gold has traditionally formed the crux of the credentials campaigns, being representative of the accolades, the product colour and taste, and even the premium value of the brand. Providing consumers with a rational reason for choosing Tiger Beer was, and continues to be, an important component of Tiger Beer's communications campaign.

The Hallmark 1 television commercial leveraged on Tiger Beer's Gold Medal achievements and reached out to viewers in Singapore, Myanmar, Cambodia and Vietnam.

REWARD FOR WINNERS WHO PERFORM NOTABLE DEEDS CAMPAIGN (MID 90s)

This is my favourite Tiger Beer TV campaign of all time. The three commercials in this campaign—Matador, Sky Rescue and Marlin—are not only truly memorable, they further strengthened Tiger Beer's position as the beer for winners.

Matador is set in a small, quiet Spanish town. Directed by

Roman Coppola (who at that time had just finished assisting his father in directing Bram Stoker's *Dracula*), the commercial starts with a little girl walking down a street and coming face to face with a bull. The bull is lowering its horns and looking to do what bulls do—charge at anyone in their paths. As the bull snorts and digs its heels into the ground, a young man sitting at a cafe jumps up, grabs a tablecloth and positions himself in front of the bull to shield the girl. He then coaxes the beast to charge at him. It charges straight through a gate and the young man closes the gate and locks the bull in. A crowd appears and cheers the matador. Someone shouts in Spanish: "Give that man a beer." And the young man replies in Spanish: "Make that a Tiger."

In Sky Rescue, two skydivers jump off a plane and one gets into trouble when the parachute fails to open. The other goes to the rescue, catches hold of the skydiver in trouble, opens his parachute and lands them safely. The skydiver who is rescued turns out to be a pretty girl—a damsel in distress always makes for a good storyline—and she is suitably grateful at being rescued.

Screen grab from the Matador commercial, aired in Singapore, Cambodia and Myanmar in the mid 90s.

A crowd gathers and cheers the hero. Someone shouts: "Give that man a beer." Very appropriate, because beer is often seen as a reward after a hard day's work. Then someone else shouts: "No! Give that man a Tiger!" Even better. Not just any beer, but a Tiger Beer. That is the message for beer drinkers. Brilliant advertising!

THE QUEST (2002)

This commercial was produced during the period of decentralisation of Tiger Beer's advertising campaigns. It looks very much like a premium Chinese pugilist movie—yes, it is that well executed. In fact, at the time The Quest was launched, I thought it was far superior to many Chinese movies of that genre. It was only used in Southeast Asia, which I thought was strange since it would have ideally suited the Asian mystique aura that Tiger Beer had going for it in its Western markets. Still, I enjoyed The Quest very much.

The commercial opens in ancient China. A young woman is captured by enemy troops whose leader is a tall and sinister looking man. A young soldier from the other side is also captured but he manages to overpower his captors and grabs a sword. That starts a duel with the enemy leader. An epic struggle ensues. The scene then fast-forwards to 20th-century New York, where the young soldier is now dressed in modern-day clothes and is hailing a taxi. Lo and behold, across the street, stands the modern-day version of his nemesis. They fight for the taxi. A chase ensues. The young man escapes and enters a bar where his date—the same lady from the ancient China scene—is waiting for him. She is upset with him but he simply smiles at her, takes a sip of his Tiger Beer and says: "Heavy traffic."

The Quest also played on Tiger Beer's positioning as the beer for winners. It is dramatic and entertaining, and it paved the way for the current "Tiger Ten" TV commercial that is probably the most cinematic beer commercial ever produced.

PARADE (2003)

This commercial continued the theme of "Good As Gold Around The World" by using more gold imagery. It also introduced the new slogan, "It's Time". The message? It is time to get a Tiger Beer and there is no other time that is as perfect for a taste of the award winning Tiger Beer as the present.

WHAT TIME IS IT? (2004)

This commercial has a very local flavour. It features a group of men in various scenes trying to get out of whatever they are doing to join their friends at a bar for a Tiger Beer. It isn't a particularly strong commercial as it does not differentiate Tiger Beer enough and makes Tiger Beer look too mainstream. Take away the Tiger Beer name and logo, and it could have been a commercial for any other beer. Tiger Beer is a beer for winners but this campaign showed grown men having to sneak out from their homes (to get away from their wives) and from work to have a beer. It smacks of truancy, which is hardly the image of a winner.

STAR (2005)

This is the one commercial that did not go down well with viewers. It scored quite badly in the regular advertising recall tests that Tiger Beer undertakes to measure the effectiveness of its advertising campaigns. It was the first time that Tiger Beer used a Hollywood star in its TV commercials but I think they chose the wrong actress in Jessica Alba. Someone with a lot more attitude and edge like Angelina Jolie might have worked better. This is, after all, an edgy

Asian beer and Angelina Jolie likes things Asian. Having said that, Jessica Alba probably resonated with young adults because of her appearance in the movie *Fantastic Four*.

The commercial begins in a hotel with three men who chance on a poster giving details of a press conference with Jessica Alba. One of them says to his friend: "Jessica Alba. Isn't that your favourite actress?" The men venture into the conference room to see her only to find it packed. The fan looks a bit disheartened but his friends have an idea. They enter a control room and open a bottle of Tiger Beer in front of the microphone. Upon hearing the sound, everyone in the conference room begins to feel the urge for a beer. One of the friends then announces: "Enjoy ice cold Tiger Beer in the lobby bar." Everyone rushes out of the room. Just then, Jessica Alba enters the room and is puzzled to see only one person there. The fan raises his hand and Jessica says: "Yes?" He asks her: "How about a Tiger Beer?"

She agrees and they go into the control room where they drink some Tiger Beer. Jessica accidentally pushes a button that turns on a camera in the room and projects her image onto a large screen in the lobby bar. When she finishes her beer, she turns to the three men and says: "Who's going to get me another Tiger?" A waiter who is about to serve a bottle to a guest in the lobby bar sees her asking for the beer on the screen and decides to rush that beer to her so that he can meet her. And that is where the commercial ends.

Now, I do not know what this commercial is trying to say to me. The message is not clear and this is a case where somebody did not quite figure out what to say before saying it. What made the commercial worse was that it did not appear real and the actors were not natural.

WINNING CAMPAIGN (2006)

This is Tiger Beer back on form! In fact, Tiger Beer came back with a vengeance with its latest TV commercial campaign called "Tiger: Unravel The Secret", which the Tiger Beer people fondly call "Tiger Ten". The previous two campaigns were rather lacklustre but this one really blows your mind away even though you may need to watch it several times to fully appreciate the entire story. Shot on location in Prague and accompanied by an original score, "Tiger: Unravel The Secret" is a five-part short film (each 60 to 90 seconds long) that weaves a story around Tiger Beer's history and the extraordinary number of awards that it has won since its humble beginnings in 1932.

The story revolves around a mysterious group of ten men who go to great lengths to protect the secret of Tiger Beer's success from an envious cartel that is pursuing them relentlessly across different countries and eras—Asia (1939), London (1954), Paris (1979) and New York (2004). The series begins with a prelude—a trailer that captures the characters and the flavours of the story—which whets the audience's appetite for the subsequent four parts that follow. Spanning decades, cities and cinematic styles, each part takes the audience on an epic adventure as award winning Director Derin Seale created intrigue and brought the film to a level of what he calls 'classic believability' via tonally excellent production design and state-of-the-art camera techniques.

While the characters may be a dramatisation, the awards and Tiger Beer's provenance showcased in the film along with its worldwide recognition, popularity and success are real. (In fact, this is where some confusion was caused in Singapore with some Tiger Beer drinkers wondering if the awards were real!) This TV commercial breaks new ground in brand communications as it collaborates with gurus in the film making and brand communications industry to release what Tiger Beer embraces as the beer industry's first Hollywood-style short film—Derin Seale; John Seale, Director of Photography (he won an Oscar for cinematography for *The English Patient*); and Linda Locke, Gold Cannes Lion winner and Regional Executive Creative Director of Leo Burnett Asia Pacific.

Created for Tiger Beer's home and regional markets, the commercial adds depth to the brew's premium status in Asia, especially in home ground Singapore and in the stronghold markets of Vietnam and Cambodia, among others. It adopts a totally unique approach to deliver distinctive facets of Tiger Beer that have not been emphasised in previous brand communications campaigns. It is a milestone effort indeed, one that epitomises Tiger Beer's tradition of excellence and world acclaimed status. The commercial is designed to catapult Tiger Beer to the pinnacle of brand communications as it entertains viewers with an air of mystery, suspense and adventure while the plot to discover the highly coveted 'secret' to Tiger Beer's success unfolds.

To Dr Les Buckley, Director of Group Commercial, Asia Pacific Breweries Limited, the commercial veers away from the traditional approach to beer brand communications. It offers a creative answer to consumers' growing interest in Tiger Beer's history and heritage while the short film format is effective in showcasing four of Tiger's most significant milestones. "Our worldwide research indicated that consumers are increasingly finding the Tiger Beer story a compelling one. It is unheard of for an Asian beer to have won so many awards in Europe which is at the heart of beer making. As such, we are inspired to tell Tiger Beer's story in the most interesting and engaging way. Since a good story deserves a great telling, we believe the short film will be a differentiating format welcomed by consumers. In an increasingly competitive global market, the short film will be more than just a piece of distinctive Tiger Beer communications. It is also set to continue the brand's tradition of successful blockbuster campaigns," said Dr Buckley.

More significantly, "Tiger: Unravel The Secret" is leading a new and niche genre of brand driven initiatives that is set to generate a buzz in the brand communications industry. Adding to the comments on the world class team, Ms Locke said: "To conceptualise, script and bring to fruition a series of films of this calibre always need a world class creative team. At Leo Burnett, we did something considered radical in our industry. We asked nine creative teams from around our global network to come back with their ideas. We wanted to have a global perspective from award winning art directors and copywriters. Among the ideas that came back to me, we found the one we were looking for from our Sydney office and developed it as a cross-market team with Mark Collis, National Executive Creative Director of Leo Burnett Australia. We then worked with Tiger to ensure that we collaborated with a crew eminent in the movie world. Once the crew was in place, we knew we were set to deliver a truly cinematic experience—on TV, in cinema and on the Internet."

"Tiger: Unravel The Secret" took nine months to complete, not including the many man hours spent trawling through countless old Tiger documents and newspaper reports which contributed to the storyboard. Time was also spent talking to veterans of Tiger Beer whose unrecorded tales of the lager's early history further inspired the plot development of the short film.

If you have not seen the commercial, you can log on to www.unravelthesecret.com to view it. But bear in mind that by the time you read this book, the campaign might have concluded and the site taken offline. That is why you need to thank the folks at YouTube where you can check out the commercial.

TASTE IT IN THIS LIFE CAMPAIGN (2006)

In 2006, Tiger Beer also released a fantastic commercial called Reincarnation. Meant to be a viral campaign, it was not shown on television but was circulated among the public via the e-mail. The viral featured a man crossing a street to get a Tiger Beer, only to be run down by a lorry. He finds himself reincarnated as an animal. Frustrated at not being able to get his beer, he dies several times in the hope of being reincarnated as a human being so that he gets to drink the beer. The viral won a Gold Medal that year at the Cannes Film Festival.

ROADBLOCKS

THE DARK MARKETS

For those countries that have banned alcohol advertising altogether, Tiger Beer has a rather sinister-sounding term for them—Dark Markets. Such countries currently are Azerbaijan, Bahrain, Finland, France, Hungary, Iceland, India, Indonesia, Jordan, Kazakhstan, Kuwait, Malaysia, Mexico, Mongolia, Norway, Russia, Sri Lanka, Sweden, Switzerland, Syria, Thailand, Venezuela and Vietnam, which is expected to go dark soon as the bill to ban beer advertising has just been tabled.

Among the Dark Markets that Tiger Beer is currently being brewed in are Malaysia, Mongolia, Thailand and Vietnam. The advertising ban created much difficulty in marketing the beer,

HATAY

CHINA

LAOS

THAILAND

CAMBODIA

HO CHI MINH CITY

especially since beer (and cigarettes) relies heavily on advertising for its brand communications. Tiger Beer needed to find other means of reaching out to consumers. And here is the irony of it all. In these Dark Markets, Tiger Beer managed to generate a lot of publicity in the press by moving away from traditional methods of using above-the-line advertising (such as print advertisements, TV and radio commercials) to below-the-line methods to communicate the brand. The latter refers to public relations, events, road shows, guerilla marketing, direct marketing and web marketing.

Getting around the problem posed by the Dark Markets was not the reason why Tiger Beer launched below-the-line activities. Tiger Beer was being progressive. It is always looking for new ways and new platforms to communicate the brand and connect with its customers. It wants to create a strong emotional bond, and the alternative (and may I say, very innovative) platforms that Tiger Beer created have certainly paid off. In this day and age of the Internet and more specifically, YouTube, you can still post a really catchy TV commercial online and then use word of mouth to get people to watch it. The fact that the commercial is illegal for public broadcast in a Dark Market will make more people want to watch it. And after watching it, they will probably tell their friends or e-mail them about it. It is just human nature, after all. The more you ban something, the more people are curious about it.

This is part of viral marketing and is one effective way of getting around the problem of Dark Markets. Create a really cool TV commercial and get people to circulate it around. Post it on YouTube and on blogs, and make a big deal of its illegal nature. People will flock to watch it. You know what they say: "Forbidden fruit always tastes sweeter."

TIGER BEER, FOOTBALL AND TIGER FC

I do not know why this is so but beer has always been associated with sports. When people watch sports, they usually do so in the company of a beer and often their friends. Beer and sports are inseparable, so it seems. It is the same with football. More than any other sport, I think football has the largest following outside of the United States where a different kind of football is played.

In Singapore, Malaysia, Thailand and Vietnam—Tiger Beer's key Asian markets—football is big. Tiger Beer's surveys reveal that football has the largest mindshare among all the sports in these countries. In Singapore, the English Premier League (EPL) has a mindshare of 48 per cent. In Malaysia, it is 30 per cent. In Thailand, it is a whopping 70 per cent.

Tiger Beer wanted to associate the brand with football to increase its mindshare. That is a smart move because people who watch football drink more beer than non-football fans. That was what Tiger Beer found out in its surveys. So, if you associate yourself with football, you are not just increasing the profile of your brand, you are reaching out to people who drink beer. And to do this, Tiger Beer needed a cohesive and coordinated platform to spearhead this part of its branding efforts.

Tiger Beer has had a long association with football in this region. In the mid to late 90s, it sponsored the Singapore S-League competition and the Tiger Fives international futsal competition. For nine years, from 1996 to 2005, it sponsored the popular Tiger Cup. Tiger Beer sponsors football because the sport is popular in Asia, it is a team sport, and it is a great natural platform for social networking. Just as importantly, the sport is masculine, like the brew.

In this screen grab from a television commercial aired regionally in 2004 and 2005, Tiger Beer was broadcast sponsor of ESPN Star Sports' coverage of the Barclays English Premier League.

THE TIGER CUP

Tiger Beer was the title sponsor for the Tiger Cup since its inception in 1996. Organised by the ASEAN Football Federation, the Tiger Cup was a biannual regional football competition contested by the national teams of nations in Southeast Asia. The cup was won three times by both Singapore and Thailand. Indonesia was runner-up three times but has never won the cup. Malaysia and Vietnam were also runners-up once each. The Tiger Cup has become a symbol of football prowess in Southeast Asia.

Although football has long been regarded as the ASEAN region's most popular sport, the introduction of the Tiger Cup brought even greater attention to the sport and showcased the passion that is felt for the game throughout the region. As the only regional football competition to feature the full 'A' national teams of the ASEAN nations, the Tiger Cup has firmly supplanted the SEA Games, which is now contested at the under-23 level.

So, why did Tiger Beer end its sponsorship of the Tiger Cup in 2005? Well, as popular as the Tiger Cup was, it was a biannual event. Tiger Beer needed something that was more regular so as to keep the brand in the spotlight longer and with greater frequency. It also needed something that was more high profile and watched by more football fans. The EPL was ideal. Tiger Beer has been sponsoring the live telecast of EPL matches for the past few years. And it also sponsors two top European football supporters' clubhouses in Singapore and other ASEAN countries—Arsenal FC and FC Barcelona. This is all very good but Tiger Beer needed a platform to tie all of these together. Sponsoring the football clubs and the telecast of EPL matches is great but sponsorships come and go. Tiger Beer needed something that would help the brand build an emotional bridge between Tiger Beer and football fans.

Above: Screen grab from Soccer Mania television commercial aired regionally in 2005 and 2006. Opposite: A Tiger FC button.

TIGER FC

Enter Tiger FC, a club for hardcore football fans to come together and discuss football while enjoying a Tiger Beer. Tiger FC was designed to get Tiger Beer closer to football fans. Tiger Beer people are passionate about football and that was why they created the Tiger FC platform. Tiger FC even has its own charter, which reads as follows:

> Welcome to Tiger FC. Please leave small talk and polite conversation at the door. In this club, winning isn't part of the game. It is the game. The members of Tiger FC don't clap politely and say "hard luck" when some loser finds only the cross bar from a position even your mum could score from. They don't smile forgivingly when a hopeless defender scores an own goal. Within the club, any wimpy remarks such as "It's all about sportsmanship" or "Everybody's a winner" will qualify you for an early bath. So, if you don't have anything worthwhile to say, you might as well keep it shut.
>
> If we find you sitting on the fence with regard to the team you're rooting for, we reserve the right to kindly kick your behind. Should you be seen drinking anything other than Tiger Beer, you will be issued a warning. If you drink anything from a cocktail glass with a small pink umbrella in it, you're red carded. Drinking Tiger Beer, however, will take you straight to the core of the action. Before you know it, you're top of the league. It's all about the thirst. And remember, 100% isn't good enough.

Well, with a charter like that, Tiger FC is obviously the club for hardcore football fans, or those who think they are. Tiger FC even has its own TV commercials showing spoofs of real football scenes, such as football players being given a tongue lashing or taking a dive in the changing room and blaming it on the other player. The commercials end with the line "Real Fans Understand" and the

voice-over says: "World acclaimed Tiger Beer brings you Tiger FC, the home of real fans." Tiger FC also sponsors other football related TV programmes that bring viewers behind the scenes to give a firsthand account of what is happening in the world of football. Here are some of the benefits that Tiger FC members get:

- Big game atmosphere. Big screens. Big crowd. All of these at Tiger FC outlets, of which there are some 30 in Singapore.
- Member discounts at Tiger FC outlets.
- Entry and VIP seating for members and their friends on match days.
- Chance to win merchandise and a Tiger FC Home Game where members bring the crowd and Tiger Beer will bring the beer, the big screen and more action right to their home.
- Regular SMSes, e-mails and newsletters.
- Updates on Tiger FC and football.
- Football news.

Tiger FC was first launched in 2004 in a Dark Market—Malaysia. This was followed by two other Dark Markets—Thailand and Vietnam—and finally Singapore. When Tiger FC was launched in Thailand in 2005, 3,500 people turned out for the launch event even though there was no advertising. In 2007, Tiger FC membership boasts some 26,000 fans.

Is the strategy working in terms of marketing the brand? I would have to say yes because Tiger Beer has top of the mind recall in these markets. In Malaysia, it is 47 per cent. And the more important thing is that Tiger FC generates a lot of publicity for the brand in the media and through word of mouth. To top it all off, 78 per cent of Tiger FC members drink beer at least once in a month compared to the general public where only 39 per cent drink beer at least once in the same time period. Check out Tiger FC's website at www.tigerfc.com.

GOING THE ROAD LESS TRAVELLED

TIGER TRANSLATE

Tiger Translate is another unconventional brand communications platform that Tiger Beer developed to promote the brand. This extremely useful tool has allowed Tiger Beer to generate plenty of publicity in the media, even in the Dark Markets. The reason for all that publicity is that Tiger Translate is not just about beer. It is about something higher. The idea originated from Tiger Beer's New Zealand office in 2005.

The concept is very simple. Tiger Beer has always been the Asian beer that has won the world over. It has over 40 international beer competition medals in its trophy room. And it is the Asian beer that has successfully crossed over to the West. It is now accepted in both the East and West as a quality beer. Tiger Beer wanted to build on this heritage with Tiger Translate, a platform to help emerging artists, film makers, designers, photographers and musicians in Asia express themselves better in the hope that one day, they too can be world acclaimed. It is a noble goal indeed.

Tiger Translate organises events that showcase these Asian talents in the world's trendiest cities such as Shanghai, Dublin, Auckland, New York, Beijing, Dubai, and more cities are being lined up even as this book is written. The rallying cry is: "Tiger Beer brings the best of Asia to the West." Tiger Translate events are

Phunk Studio's graphic designers. From left: William Chan, Jackson Tan, Alvin Tan and Melvin Chee.

never marketed the conventional way. Guerilla marketing tactics are employed—posters, invites, e-mails, word of mouth, MySpace, YouTube, blogs and so on. It seems to have worked very well. Tiger Translate events are always packed with people. And of course, the brew of choice is always Tiger Beer.

The launch event in Shanghai was estimated to have reached 4 million people through the media publicity that was created. Now in its second year, Tiger Translate has worked with the likes of Phunk Studio, Faile, Rostarr and many more rising Asian stars. Creating events in Dublin, Shanghai and Auckland last year proved to be a solid foundation to move into another year of creative enlightenment and entertainment.

For Tiger Beer's 75th anniversary celebrations, it has identified 75 emerging Asian artists to feature at Tiger Translate events throughout the world. These events are estimated to have generated some S$5.6 million in free publicity for Tiger Beer. To date, more than 32 million people have been exposed to Tiger Translate. Here is a sampling of what media people have been saying about Tiger Translate.

"With Translate, Tiger is setting the stage for other brands to follow."
– *John Lee, Theme Magazine*

"I think Tiger Beer is getting a new essence of youth injected into the brand and that's great."
– *Angelia Seetoh, Editor, Designer Magazine*

"It's great that the works of so many emerging Asian artists are featured in this leading design city. Through the Tiger Translate showcase, our emerging Asian artists are given the opportunity to display their talents to a wider international audience and garner future prospects."
– *Chris Ng, Producer, International Designers' Network (IdN)*

"Tiger Translate is a great platform. It's the first that we know of that showcases emerging Asian artists and that's excellent."
– *Daniel Jackson, Surface to Air, New York*

"I think this is the best thing that a brand can do if it wants to get its name spread out."
– *Tobias Rapp, Cultural Editor In Chief, Taz, Berlin*

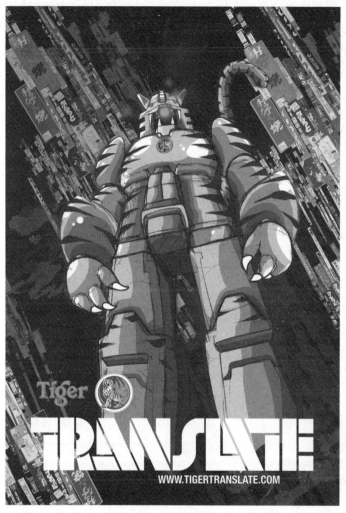

A Tiger Translate poster created by Eric Chan.

"I'm glad I had the opportunity to be a part of this showcase. Asia has always fascinated me and to have an event like this brought to Berlin, gives people here a glimpse into Asia through the artworks."

– Tiger AKA Jans Rikus Hillman, co-founder of leading art magazine De bug. Rikus also designed the cover of the 'Rise' book and promotional collaterals for Tiger Translate Berlin.

"To me, Tiger Translate Berlin was like a boat ride that brought the guests to Asia and back. While talking to guests at the event, I found that they were impressed by what they saw in the Asian artworks. Tiger Translate Berlin was a success in providing Berliners with an insight into the work of Asian artists and a first hand glimpse into Asia."

– Lin Yu, Journalist from City Pictorial (China)

"I think it's a good way to bring the brand to the people."

– Isabelle Spilker, Art Editor, Blond Magazine, Hamburg

It looks like Tiger Beer has created an effective platform that is highly scalable to communicate the brand. And this platform is set to grow in the coming years. The idea is to decentralise the event. Currently, everything is organised and funded by the head office in Singapore but moving forward, each operating country where Tiger Beer has a branch office will take on the responsibility of organising Tiger Translate events in their own country so as to create events that are more suitable to local tastes. Tiger Translate's website is located at www.tigertranslate.com. Check it out. Words alone cannot express the feel of these events.

TIGERLIVE

On 15 December 2006, Tiger Beer unveiled TigerLIVE, Southeast Asia's first multi-sensory brand entertainment centre. Housed in the newly opened St James Power Station near Sentosa Island, TigerLIVE is a unique showcase that puts the homegrown beer on par with other internationally renowned beer brands with similar initiatives. It also showcases the brand's rich Asian heritage and award winning legacy. With TigerLIVE, Tiger Beer is crossing a new milestone in its illustrious history. TigerLIVE was launched in 2007 in conjunction with Tiger Beer's year-long celebrations to commemorate its 75th anniversary.

It took the team at Tiger Beer one and a half years to develop TigerLIVE. At an investment of S$10 million and spanning some 1,300 square metres, TigerLIVE has enthralled visitors with state-of-the-art and innovative multimedia technologies using high-tech animation effects and illusory techniques such as the Pepper's ghost effect, and the use of glass and special lighting effects which give a three-dimensional appearance to the characters and settings. Visitors embark on an interactive and seamless journey, comprising eight specially created experiences—Tiger Tales, Tiger Universe, Tiger Allure, Beginnings, Tiger Nation, Grain to Gold, Tiger Super Cold and Tiger Den—all under one roof. These areas portray the origins and legacy of Tiger Beer, including the brewing processes, innovations and its evolution from a local beer to an internationally recognisable Singapore icon—all in a fun and interactive way.

Commenting on the launch of TigerLIVE, Mr Alan Gourdie, General Manager, Asia Pacific Breweries Singapore (APBS), said: "With TigerLIVE, we hope to present The Ultimate Tiger Experience

Visitors to the Grain To Gold section at TigerLIVE enjoy an animated show about the beer's brewing process.

to our consumers. We wanted to create a popular destination for a Singapore icon and make Singaporeans proud of the local and international achievements of their homegrown beer over the past 74 years. As the first showcase by a local brand that is synonymous with Singapore, we believe that TigerLIVE is a fresh, new concept that will appeal to both local and international visitors."

Ms Andrea Teo, Head of New Business Development, APBS, provides an insight into the creative concept and development of TigerLIVE: "Constantly at the forefront of beer innovation, Tiger Beer aims to redefine consumers' expectations of the typical brewery tour and provide them with a unique, multi sensory experience. TigerLIVE signals the brand's commitment to introduce novel initiatives to enhance the Tiger experience for consumers. When TigerLIVE was first conceptualised, we wanted it to appeal to everyone—young and old, locals and foreigners. There will be something for everyone ranging from special effects for the tech savvy, its location at the trendy St James Power Station for hip consumers and enjoying a Super Cold Tiger for beer fans."

TigerLIVE is poised to become Singapore's next wave of experiential showcases for local brands and a must-see lifestyle and entertainment destination. Its proximity to some of Singapore's top attractions such as Sentosa, Mount Faber and the upcoming Resorts World at Sentosa will enable it to tap into the expected visitor arrivals of about 17 million people to Singapore annually by 2015. The TigerLIVE showcase expects to attract about 300,000 visitors in its first year of operations.

There is a section on the TigerLIVE website which talks about the best way to enjoy a beer. This is a really nice touch because it shows that Tiger Beer is passionate about beer. Let me save you the trouble of putting this book down to log into the website. The following is a reproduction of what you will find there in the "Best Practice/Tips" page. By the way, TigerLIVE's website is located at www.tigerlive.com.sg.

We all know drinking Tiger Beer is an enjoyable experience. But to fully appreciate its appearance, smell, taste and character will require some skill. So here are a few useful tips for you to note the next time you have a glass of Tiger Beer in your hand. It's time to truly savour each Tiger Beer as if it's your last.

• Shelf life
Tiger Beer does not improve with age, and is best drunk when it is fresh. The shelf life of bottled and canned beer is

guaranteed for six months. A freshly opened keg of draught Tiger Beer should be consumed within three days or earlier. An unopened keg can only be stored for a month.

• Glassware

It's important to pour Tiger Beer into a clean glass. Not only is that the best way to see the colour and head of the beer, but more importantly, it's also the only way to release the flavour, aroma and certain gasses. A dirty beer glass will cause the foam to collapse quickly, resulting in a flat beer. Certainly not very appetising if you were to drink it. You can tell a dirty glass when you see patches of bubble clinging to the inner wall of the glass after you have poured the beer in it. Also, refrain from using household detergent to clean your glass. The recommended detergent is called Diflex. [That is really great to know if you are a real beer drinker.]

• Correct temperature

The correct serving temperature should be between 4 and 6 degrees Celsius. This may seem too cold but bear in mind that beer temperature can increase very quickly in our tropical climate.

• Appearance

Before taking that first of many sips of your Tiger Beer, raise your glass and admire what's in front of you. Take a few seconds to note the beer's colour, carbonation and retention. The colour of the beer should reflect a gold yellow hue. As you check out the colour, do also take note of the top of the glass. A foamy head should form when the beer is poured.

• Good foam head

A good foam head will enhance the appeal of your Tiger Beer, thus making the beer drinking an enjoyable experience. A good foam head should be at least 2 cm high, slightly above the rim of the glass.

• Aroma

Smelling the beer gives the palate a sense of what to expect. Since the sense of smell becomes saturated quite quickly, it is important to take special note of the aromas you detect during the first smell. As you inhale, you should at first discern the dominant scent. The dominant scent is the initial aroma released during the pour, and can be a mixture of malt and hops.

• Taste

Now, it's finally time to get your taste buds on. But don't just swallow the beer. Take that first sip and let the beer linger in your mouth for a couple of seconds. Breathe through your nose as you are doing this. This process is known as "retro-olfaction", and it allows the beer's scent to reach your olfactory nerves, which, due to the connection between the senses of taste and smell, intensifies the flavour of your Tiger Beer.

• Satisfaction

So go ahead, enjoy the rest of that Tiger Beer. Now that you know what's out there, you can enjoy it to its fullest potential.

ONLINE COMMUNITY

Tiger Beer also tries to reach out to its customers and build loyalty through an online community the way MySpace and Facebook have done. Tiger Beer started not too long ago and is fully aware of the difficulty in implementing it. While MySpace and Facebook are social networking sites and can garner a much wider audience, the Tiger Beer site can only target Tiger Beer drinkers. Tiger Beer is a beer. What can you possibly talk about beer with your cyber friends? No matter how much you like Tiger Beer, you will run out of things to say after a short while. Furthermore, historical weight is against Tiger Beer. So far, I have not seen any beer brands succeeding in building a vibrant online community.

But having said that, it will not stop the Tiger Beer team from trying their best. The trick here is to go beyond beer and find something that beer drinkers can share and enjoy together. So far, the most active Tiger Beer online community is the one in the United Kingdom. Marilyn Tan heads Tiger Beer's Internet strategy. She told me that Tiger Beer United Kingdom does it by encouraging Tiger Beer drinkers to post their travel experiences on the website and share with each other on what destinations are cool and why. At first, I was rather sceptical. Do people do things like that? I would not have bothered but it's good to know there are people in the United Kingdom who care enough to share.

There is a cool page in the UK website called Tiger Beer Film Dub. Tiger Beer purchased old movies and loaded selected scenes on the website. Members logging on can dub the scenes in their own script and send them to their friends. At the time of writing, the movie that is on the Film Dub page is an old Chinese kung fu film called *Iron Monkey*.

Perhaps one of the ways to build an online community for beer drinkers is to have a forum on … what else but beer, or rather beer related activities. There are many bars, pubs, discos and karaoke lounges in Singapore. Start a forum on the Tiger Beer website where people can go to and talk about these places. Allow people to blog about their favourite haunts, maybe even post photos of themselves and their friends having a good time. I know there are other such sites in Singapore but none that is sponsored by a major brand like Tiger Beer, which is also served in most of these entertainment places.

BRAND CHAMPIONS AND BRAND AMBASSADORS

To be a successful brand, you need two types of people—brand champions and brand ambassadors. Often, the brand champion's job goes to the CEO. Strong brands need strong brand champions who live and breathe the brand every day. Look at the strongest brands in the world like Microsoft (Bill Gates), Oracle (Larry Ellison), Nike (Phil Knight), General Electric (Jack Welch), Disney (Walt Disney), Starbucks (Howard Schultz) and Ferrari (Enzo Ferrari), among others. They each have or had a strong brand champion as CEO. Some of these CEOs are no longer with the company but their legacies live on.

The brand champion's job is to inspire employees of the company to become brand ambassadors who will also live and breathe the brand in all that they do. As a company grows in terms of size and geographical markets, brand ambassadors become more and more important because without brand ambassadors, your brand will get stuck. Tiger Beer understands this need acutely, so much so that 'Brand Champion' is an official job description in Tiger Beer.

Tiger Beer has a group of young, knowledgeable and enthusiastic people who carry the title 'Brand Champion'. I have met some of them—Ray Poletti, Adam Gerard, David Lim, Marilyn Tan and Tan Jwee Peng. Their job is to develop the platforms to communicate the brand clearly around the world and in the process, create brand ambassadors within the company as well as outside. Tiger Beer has many more Brand Champions in its team around the world, all working hard towards a common goal—to take the Tiger Beer brand to the next level of growth.

Here are just some of the ground-breaking activities that the Brand Champions have done so far. In 2004, they organised the first ever Tiger Beer Chilli Crab Festival in New York. It was so successful that similar events were held in Singapore in 2006 and in London's Brick Lane in 2007. In 2004 in London, they organised an event called 16 Feet Underground, a Thai boxing competition in which eight *muay thai* boxers (16 feet, get it?) competed against each other in an underground venue. Guerilla marketing was used to publicise the event. Tiger Beer sponsored Gay Pride, Berlin in 2005, and Chinese New Year Banquets in Auckland and Sydney in 2006 and 2007 respectively to educate people on the traditions of Chinese New Year.

It looks like they are doing a great job. Keep it up, folks!

Taking Tiger Beer Into Unchartered Waters

Tiger Beer has an ambitious goal. It wants to

become the most valuable Asian beer brand. It is today among the top three Asian beers in terms of volume, brand awareness and distribution, the other two being San Miguel (Philippines) and Singha (Thailand), according to About.com.[1] Outside of Asia, Tiger Beer is definitely the premium Asian beer of choice. Let us now look at some of the figures related to Tiger Beer.

In terms of volume, Tiger Beer is No. 18 in Asia with 2 million hectolitres (hls) produced annually. These are 2006 figures but Tiger Beer would be No. 1 if the home markets of the other beers were excluded. Most beers are big in their home markets but tiny outside of them. It's a good thing that the situation is the reverse for Tiger Beer because Singapore is such a small market.

In terms of preference, Tiger Beer ranked No. 5, and in terms of awareness, No. 6, according to the Synovate Review Asian Beer Brands 2004. Not bad. But the aggressive Tiger Beer team wants to improve on those figures. In terms of distribution, Tiger Beer is available in 60 countries, more than any other Asian beer brand. And with some 30 breweries owned by Asia Pacific Breweries (APB) in 12 countries, it is also brewed in more countries than any other Asian beer. The number continues to grow.

Tiger Beer's current growth rate is about 3 per cent a year. It wants to raise this figure substantially. In order to achieve that, it will need to do several things: seek new markets that it has not yet explored, deepen its penetration in existing markets, get occasional Tiger Beer drinkers to drink more of its brew, and encourage beer surfers to prefer Tiger Beer instead.

1. http://goasia.about.com/od/food/tp/beers.htm

SEEK NEW MARKETS

Tiger Beer has done well to get to where it is today. Although it is not the No. 1 brewery in the world (that honour goes to SAB-Miller after South African Brewery bought the Milwaukee, Wisconsin-based Miller), it does not mean that Tiger Beer is not a strong brand. Many people still misunderstand what brands are all about, often confusing the size of the brand with the power of the brand. Miller may be more widely distributed than Tiger Beer but that does not necessarily mean that Miller is a stronger brand. How so?

When I was studying and later, working, in the United States, I noticed that beer drinkers would happily switch between Budweiser and Miller. Even those who drank Miller would not be terribly upset when Miller was not available. But those who drank Samuel Adams or Heineken would not drink beer if their brand was not available. (Tiger Beer was not sold in Madison, Wisconsin, where I was.) This shows you that the size of the brand is not the same as its power. Other factors, like control over the distribution channels, account for the success of fast moving consumer goods like beer.

What do I mean when I talk about the power of a brand? I am talking about whether a brand is strong in the one and only area that matters in brand building—the MINDS of its customers. A brand is simply an idea that exists in the minds of customers. That is what a brand is. If you want to be a strong brand, you need to be strong in the minds of customers. Advertising legend Walter Landor once said: "Products are made in factories but brands are created in the minds." And in order to be a strong brand in the mind, a brand must own an idea. You do not have to be a big company to be a strong brand but a strong brand, no matter how small right now, has the potential to become a big company over time.

Tiger Beer may not be the biggest but based on general observations, Tiger Beer drinkers are a pretty loyal bunch. That must mean that Tiger Beer stands for something in their minds. I drink both Heineken and Tiger Beer (admittedly more Heineken) and James Wong, the General Manager of Tiger Export International, told me that I am exactly the type of yuppie that Heineken aims for (although I don't see myself as a yuppie). When I suggest Heineken to my friends at social occasions, many of them give me a strange look and say: "Bro, we think it's time you drink a real man's drink and that is Tiger. How come you drink that sissy imported stuff?" I hardly think Heineken is sissy and I tell them that the Heineken that is sold in Singapore is brewed by the same people who brew Tiger Beer, but I think that fact just flies over their heads. And no, these friends of mine are not construction workers but professionals and executives.

Size is not the same as power. Harley-Davidson is not the biggest motorcycle manufacturer in the world but you would agree that it is a powerful brand. Apple is not the biggest computer company in the world but it is a powerful brand. Banyan Tree is not the biggest resort operator in the world but it is a powerful brand. And like it or not, Tiger Beer is a powerful brand in the minds of its customers.

Being a powerful brand that has oodles of customer loyalty is a great thing to have. It is a good start but like all good starts, it is no use if you do not use it to finish the race in the pole position. A good start is one thing but maintaining the forward momentum relentlessly is another thing altogether. It is the latter that will grow a company. Tiger Beer has had a good start. It succeeded against all odds. It overcame the handicap of being Singaporean. For the 21st century, Tiger Beer will need to use that brand power to grow.

HATAY (2003)

DANANG (2006)

WE HAVE DOUBLED
OUR VIETNAM BREWERIES TO FOUR.

HO CHI MINH CITY (1993)

TIEN GIANG (2006)

It needs to leverage on the brand that it has built to go to places where it has never been. Perhaps I should qualify that statement. Tiger Beer *could* use that brand to go to places it has never been. But it does not need to. It can just choose to defend the turf that it has conquered and remain a speciality or niche player. There is no shame in that. Like I said, the brand's power is not the same as the brand's size. Look around and you can see many big corporations that are in trouble today because they have weak brands.

However, if you have such a strong brand, wouldn't it be a shame not to leverage on it? Certainly, it would be a shame not to try and see how far that brand can be stretched. You would want to realise the full potential of the brand and grow it. That is inevitable. That desire to grow is inherent in every brand. It has a life of its own. It is independent of the people who work for the brand (these people come and go).

One of the ways for Tiger Beer to grow is to seek out new markets. At the time of writing this book, Tiger Beer is 75 years old and is sold in 60 countries. Sixty countries! Now that is quite substantial. It would represent critical mass for the brand. Tiger Beer can use that critical mass and up the pace of exports to new markets. Brands take time to build, some longer than others, but what I do know about brands is that they are like plants and animals. The ones that grow big quickly usually do not live very long. The sequoia tree takes a long time to grow to its maximum height and the sequoia lives for hundreds of years. Brands are the same. The ones that grow slowly and steadily usually grow bigger, grow stronger and live longer. Tiger Beer has been growing steadily over the past 75 years. It can pick up the pace now as it has gained critical mass.

In management, there is a school of thought that believes in the need to build up one's home market strength before one can be successful in the international scene. I once attended a presentation given by a senior executive of an internationally renowned management consultancy firm, and he recommended this strategy to Singapore companies. I tend to agree. However, this theory poses a problem for Tiger Beer because Singapore is a small market. Even if you are No. 1 in Singapore, that still makes you a tiny player because Singapore is a smaller market than say, New York or London or Shanghai. So, in order for Tiger Beer to build up home market strength, it needs to redefine what 'home market' means. I think that for a brand like Tiger Beer, it needs to consider including the surrounding markets of Malaysia, Thailand and Vietnam as part of its 'home market'. But now that Tiger Beer is strong in these expanded home markets, it can—and should—venture more aggressively into new markets to speed up its growth.

Yes, I said that brands that grow slowly and steadily can last longer but I don't see any reason why Tiger Beer cannot speed up and not compromise the brand. Tiger Beer has shown over the years that it can control its product quality and it can maintain a consistent brand image and brand communications despite needing a two-pronged brand strategy—one for Asia and one for the West. That is the key—consistency. Usually, when brands expand, quality suffers. Tiger Beer can speed up the expansion, and probably has plans to, as long as it can do so without compromising the consistency of its product quality and brand image. I believe that it can.

So, what are the new markets that Tiger Beer has in its sights? Well, any market is possible as long as people drink beer. But of course, Tiger Beer will have to choose its entry carefully. Even if

a market looks promising, it will still need to go through its usual market entry processes, which includes asking hard questions and answering them satisfactorily, questions such as:

- Is this a growth market for beer?
- If yes, how much is it expected to grow? Would it be faster than Tiger Beer's internal growth rate?
- What is the competitive landscape like? Can Tiger Beer compete?
- Will this market go dark in the near future, therefore affecting Tiger Beer's marketing?
- Do people here know or have heard about Tiger Beer?
- What are the PEST (Political, Economic, Social and Technology) challenges that Tiger Beer will face now and in the foreseeable future?
- What are the distribution channels available in the market? Are these channels tightly controlled by competitors?
- Can Tiger Beer find a suitable local partner or does it have to go in and set up its own operations?
- Where will Tiger Beer be sold?
- Does Tiger Beer have the logistics operation to support its brand?
- What is the volume that Tiger Beer can expect to sell in this new market?

GO DEEPER INTO EXISTING MARKETS

Tiger Beer can also grow by deepening its brand penetration in existing markets. Other than Singapore, Malaysia, Vietnam and possibly Thailand, I think there is a lot more room for growth in Tiger Beer's other markets. But this is easier said than done because of two sticky issues—the dilution of the brand's power and conquest sales.

DILUTION OF THE BRAND'S POWER

In the West, Tiger Beer is seen as a hip, trendy, cool, premium beer brand with a lot of Far East mystique. That makes it attractive to the with-it crowd. Tiger Beer has been an extremely focused brand so far in the West, taking pains to carefully control how it sells the beer, where it sells the beer and to whom it sells the beer. This was purposefully done to cultivate the kind of image that other beer brands would kill for.

As a brand expands, there is the danger of diluting the brand's power through a blurring of its focus. An important rule of branding—you need FOCUS to build a strong brand. When you focus, you become good at what you do. More importantly, other people think that you are good at what you do because that is all that you do. That is why people often give more credit to specialists than they are sometimes due.

However, focus also requires one thing that many brands are not willing to do—SACRIFICE. The difference between a strong brand and a weak one is that the strong one is usually willing to sacrifice nine out of ten markets in order to be able to dominate one. A weak brand is usually weak because it tries to be everything to everyone. It tries to get its foot in every single market. That only blurs the focus of the brand and this blurred focus will result in a weaker brand.

This is a very real danger for Tiger Beer. Rapid expansion could dilute the brand's power. Tiger Beer is strong in the West because Tiger Beer was willing to sacrifice the mass market to be strong in the premium sector for hip, young people. If everybody is drinking Tiger Beer—young and old, cool and uncool, white- and blue-collar workers—that could eventually weaken Tiger Beer's hold in the mind.

However, this is not to say that Tiger Beer cannot expand the sales of its brew in existing markets like the West and still maintain its brand power at the same time. Tiger Beer can expand rapidly if it can keep the things that made it famous, the things that define what it is, unchanged. In the Western markets like the United States and the United Kingdom, for example, Tiger Beer is famous for being a cool, hip, trendy premium beer. It should maintain this and use this to expand the market. You see, there are two types of people who buy cool brands—cool people and people who want to be cool. Yes, there is still the danger of diluting Tiger Beer's brand if fat, sloppy, uncool men in their fifties start buying Tiger Beer in droves but that is something that can only be minimised, not completely eliminated. If business is without risk, then anyone can do it. What Tiger Beer is trying to do is to become an aspirational brand that people who aspire to be cool will want to be associated with.

CONQUEST SALES—NOT THE EASIEST THING

There are two ways to increase your sales in an existing market. The first way is to bank on a rapidly growing population but these days, with declining birth rates and all, the population in developed countries is not increasing that fast. It is ageing yes, but increasing, no. The second way is through conquest sales. This means that in order for you to gain a sale, somebody else will have to lose a sale. What would you do if I were to come into your market and try to take away your customers? You would fight like mad to retain them, wouldn't you?

That is the situation that Tiger Beer is facing in its existing markets, both in the West and in Asia. For Tiger Beer to gain sales, somebody else will have to lose sales. Furthermore, these markets are fairly mature and well established, with plenty of seasoned players who will try to block Tiger Beer's advance. I would be disappointed if they did not. That would have been a bad marketing move on the part of Tiger Beer's competitors. Any strategy that is conceived in a vacuum without taking into consideration the likely competitive counter-moves will probably fail.

To go head to head with the entrenched competitors in these markets the conventional way, via big budget advertising, would probably drain Tiger Beer of its resources very quickly. But I like what Tiger Beer is doing at the moment to gain market share—it is going around the mountain instead of trying to climb the mountain. I discussed earlier the unconventional marketing techniques that the brand has developed, such as Tiger FC, TigerLIVE and Tiger Translate. These are good techniques as they are less expensive and they are effective, having generated a lot of publicity in the media and via word-of-mouth marketing. Tiger Beer could use more of such clever marketing strategies to get around their entrenched competitors.

These competitors could respond in kind, however, which is why Tiger Beer must have the first mover advantage and then press this advantage home. It needs to exploit the first mover advantage to establish the brand in the only place that matters—the minds of the beer drinking population. These guerilla marketing strategies are still in their infancy but Tiger Beer has plans to ratchet up their efforts a few levels in the coming years. I will be watching with great interest. You should too.

WITH THE ADDITION OF **LAOS**
OUR FOOTPRINT IN INDOCHINA IS NOW COMPLETE.

VIETNAM

LAOS

CAMBODIA

GET OCCASIONAL TIGER BEER DRINKERS TO DRINK MORE OF THE BREW

In today's politically correct age, this ancient marketing technique of getting existing customers to use more of your product may come across as unethical. It is a Catch 22 situation. If Tiger Beer succeeds in getting existing customers to drink more, it will sell more beer but at the same time, it might lead some of these customers down the slippery slope to alcoholism. If the company is selling organic food, that might not be such a bad thing but it is selling beer, and although beer has health benefits due to the fact that it is made from malt barley and hops (and it only has 5 per cent alcohol by volume), it is still an alcoholic beverage.

But the fact of the matter is that it is six times more expensive to acquire a new customer than it is to retain an existing one. And the marketing people know that fact. It is therefore easier to get existing customers to buy more from you. However, there is a fine line between increasing sales in a reasonable manner and being seen as a heartless corporation out to exploit the public. You might have heard or read stories in business magazines about American liquor companies targeting inner city teenage kids because their research showed that these kids are the most likely to become heavy users of their products. That kind of bad press can damage or kill a brand.

So, how do you overcome this twin challenge of getting your existing customers to drink more and yet still be seen as a responsible company? Have you heard of the 80/20 rule? Twenty per cent of your customers account for 80 per cent of your sales. That is generally true. Now, for the 20 per cent of Tiger Beer's heavy users, I think there is no need to increase their consumption of beer. But for the other 80 per cent, I believe that if they drink a few more cans of Tiger Beer, it would still be all right, still within safe limits. So, there is room for growth with this 80 per cent. How do you run marketing programmes that target the 80 per cent of light users without affecting the 20 per cent of heavy users? Good question. But it is one that I do not have the answer to. Tiger Beer has a very passionate and capable marketing team behind the brand. This is a challenge for them, but I am sure they know the answer to this one as they live and breathe the brand.

ENCOURAGE BEER SURFERS TO SWITCH TO TIGER BEER

You know, a lot of people drink beer the way they watch TV—they surf the channels. Many beer drinkers switch from brand to brand. To them, beer is beer is beer. And even beer experts tell me that after the second beer, all beers taste the same. I have not had the chance to test this theory out yet because my wife won't let me have more than two. If you can get these beer surfers to prefer Tiger Beer, now that would increase your sales a fair bit. Again, building loyalty among beer drinkers who drink whatever is available or buy whatever is on sale is not an easy thing to do. Again, I do not have all the answers.

Winning Against The Odds

Every brand faces challenges as it grows and starts to expand out of the comfort zone

of its home market. Tiger Beer is no different. And the challenges that face Tiger Beer are different from market to market although there are some challenges that are the same across markets.

BEER DOES NOT TRAVEL WELL

Probably the biggest challenge facing Tiger Beer is its small home market, which has forced it to look beyond the shores of Singapore. The small domestic market is a problem that every Singapore company will eventually face as they hit their growth ceiling but it is more acutely felt by Tiger Beer. Why?

To answer that question, we have to look to the roots of beer. Beer has been around for some 2,000 years but it is not a beverage that travels well and until the invention of modern packaging techniques, beer could not be transported. It was therefore traditionally brewed at source, where people would drink it. Beer spoils quite easily too. Unlike wine, which can improve with age, beer is best drunk when fresh. It is also quite easy to brew so in most markets, Tiger Beer would face a lot of entrenched local competitors. Beer is also very expensive to transport because it is bulky and of low value. One carton of beer may weigh 8 kilograms but its value is only around S$10. Factor in transportation costs and import taxes, and beer becomes very expensive. That is why imported beers have no choice but to take the premium position even if they are priced dirt-cheap in their home country.

All these factors combine to make beer very much a local beverage. As a result, when you venture into any market that has a beer brewing industry, you will find that the local brands are usually very big. In China, Tsingtao is bigger than the imports. In the Philippines, San Miguel is bigger than the imports. In Thailand, Singha is bigger than the imports. In Indonesia, Bintang is bigger than the imports. In Japan, Kirin is bigger than the imports. In the United States, Budweiser is bigger than the imports. In Canada, Labatt is bigger than the imports—bet you have never heard of Labatt!

Most of the large local brands remain relatively local because beer does not travel well, but almost every beer brand in the world has a much larger domestic market than Tiger Beer. That puts Tiger Beer in a difficult position. Beer is a volume game since its value is low compared to hard liquors and wines. Singapore is a small market so Tiger Beer is forced to export, and when they export, they run into deeply entrenched local beer brands that have such a strong stranglehold on local beer drinkers that Tiger Beer had no choice but to become a niche player. But even being a niche player has its intractable problems.

First, the good news. Beer may not travel well but at least Tiger Beer has a name that travels well compared to many other beer brands. The tiger is an Asian animal so people can immediately identify Tiger Beer as an Asian beer, but the name is also an English name so it would be easy for most people in the West to pronounce it. And the beauty of the name is that it does not tie the brew down to a particular country. It does not say that Tiger Beer is a Singapore beer—that would be a serious handicap. However, it does say Tiger Beer is Asian and that is exactly what Tiger Beer wanted. It wanted to occupy the niche of the cool Asian beer. Tiger equals Asian and all the attendant mystique and coolness that comes with it. That works fine in the West where Tiger Beer's main competition will be other premium imports.

However, that strategy is not feasible in Asia because when Tiger Beer takes the position of the cool Asian beer, beer drinkers will probably say: "What's the big deal? There are so many local beer brands here and they are all Asian! So what's so special about Tiger Beer? It's just another beer." We have discussed Tiger Beer's "World Acclaimed" strategy for Asia so we will not spend time on that issue here. Because beer does not travel well, Tiger Beer decided to move its breweries as close as possible to its export markets. However, that is an extremely risky venture as breweries can cost tens of millions of dollars to build. The Tiger Beer brewery in Tuas, Singapore, cost S$200 million. So, Tiger Beer has to be careful where it locates its breweries.

Tiger Beer is stuck between a rock and a very hard place. It has a small domestic market, so it has to export. But it is exporting a product that does not travel well, so it will either have to be a niche premium player or build breweries in its export markets. Still, these are things that Tiger Beer has to do to fuel its expansion.

ONE MAN'S MEAT IS ANOTHER MAN'S POISON

Tiger Beer also discovered that an attribute of the brand that is seen as strength in one market can be perceived as a weakness in another market. For example, Tiger Beer's taste has always been regarded by its fans as crisp and premium, that is, having a strong and full flavour. The fact that beer experts around the world have awarded Tiger Beer over 40 awards is testament to that. Unfortunately, that was of no help in China. Chinese beer drinkers

do not perceive Tiger Beer as a strong brand as compared to the American Budweiser, in large part because of its more bitter taste. Apparently, the Chinese prefer something less bitter, which is why Tiger Beer launched the lighter tasting Tiger Crystal.

Tiger Beer had two options to deal with this challenge in China. One, modify the taste of the brew to suit local taste buds the way Coca-Cola modifies its taste from market to market. But Tiger Beer knows that this will lead to inconsistency. Two, launch a lighter beer and keep the original for those customers who prefer the bitter taste as there are surely such customers even in China. They chose the second option.

Unfortunately, Tiger Beer was quite late into the market and that allowed Budweiser to gain ground. Budweiser's taste is lighter, so light that to me it is almost tasteless. A German pal I once shared a flat with in the United States used to tell me that American beer must be drunk really cold because the taste is so weak. Well, I've not had a Budweiser in 13 years and I do not know if they have changed the formula but what is tasteless to a German drinker might be wonderful to a Chinese drinker. Taste is a very subjective matter but as we can see from Tiger Beer's experience in China, it would have an impact on market share.

The Tiger Crystal is an exception that Tiger Beer made due to the demands of its Chinese customers. This is the first and only time Tiger Beer line-extended its brand. So far, Tiger Crystal has had a positive impact and helped Tiger Beer enjoy a net increase in sales. One strategy that Tiger Beer could consider if Tiger Crystal continues to grow rapidly is to make it the main brand for China and phase out Tiger Beer slowly. But this is a move that requires careful consideration.

THE COMPETITION IS NOT JUST OTHER BEER BRANDS

When venturing into overseas markets, every brand will face stiff competition. Tiger Beer's competition does not come from just other beer brands alone but also from other alcoholic beverages like whisky and brandy. In China, hard liquors are popular at entertainment outlets and are seen as more high class compared to even premium international beers. These drinking habits and preferences are hard to change. Beer brands are feeling the heat from hard liquors. Not only that, there is also the aggressive local competition to consider. In China, for instance, local brands like Tsingtao, Yanjing, Snow and Zhujiang have premium versions of their beer that are selling very well in their home country.

Although drinking habits are hard to change, they sometimes do, whether as a result of a pioneering brand aggressively promoting a particular category of alcoholic beverage (such as Miller promoting the light beer category in the United States with its famous tag line "Tastes Great, Less Filling" to imply that because it is light, you can drink more of it) or due to other reasons. Mongolia is a vodka drinking country but Tiger Beer observed that there is a trend towards beer and it is readying itself to take advantage of this expected shift. Since beer is relatively new to Mongolian drinkers and there are no established brands there yet, Tiger Beer has a chance to be the No. 1 brand there. It does not matter if Budweiser or Miller is bigger than Tiger Beer. This is considered a green field area and any brand can become No. 1.

I would like to draw your attention to the ill-fated Volkswagen Phaeton. According to most test reports that I have read, this is an impressive car—well engineered, refined, smooth, well built and competitively priced. It was designed to compete in the upper echelons of the luxury car market against the likes of the Mercedes-Benz S Class, BMW 7 Series, Audi A8, Lexus LS600h and Jaguar XJ8. But it was doomed to fail right from the start. Why? Because people who intend to buy a luxury car like this will have the preconceived notion that it must carry a certain badge, and Volkswagen is just not the kind of badge they want in a luxury car. The Volkswagen Phaeton also shared its platform with the Volkswagen Touareg SUV but the Touareg was better received than the Phaeton. Why? The Touareg is competing in a category called *luxury SUVs* and since most people buying a luxury SUV are buying it for the first time, the brand is less critical. That is why the Lexus RX330 is the best selling luxury SUV in the United States.

Tiger Beer is in the same situation in Mongolia. It may not be the biggest brand in beer globally but Mongolia is akin to the luxury SUV category in that it really does not matter. However, speed is still of essence. Tiger Beer has to move fast to establish the brand in the minds of customers in Mongolia before any other brand. This will require a massive injection of funds initially. The way to dominate a category is at the stage when it is starting to form, not after it has matured. When the computer category was still in its infancy, IBM saw its potential. The computer category at that time was akin to the luxury SUV. IBM dropped everything else to focus on computers and it got into the market early. It established the brand in the mind firmly. And it won big. Tiger Beer may need to make a similar move depending on its assessment of the potential of the market. If it really thinks that there will be a move from vodka to beer, then the time to capture this emerging category is now.

To make matters worse, it is apparently very expensive to market beer in China, especially in big cities like Shanghai where the media costs rival that of Singapore's. So, Tiger Beer has decided that it will give Tiger Crystal a try and take the sniper approach to its China marketing—sell only in selected cities and use guerilla marketing to penetrate the market. The original Tiger Beer brew will be available and targeted at the expatriates, while Tiger Crystal will be aimed at the younger local drinkers in their twenties.

Another strategy is to again narrow the focus. Since Tiger Beer does not have the resources of brands like Budweiser and the local brands, it could narrow its focus to an area that it can dominate. One such area is draught beer (or tap beer). For some reason, Tiger Beer is generally regarded as the best draught beer in China, and is No. 1 in cities like Shanghai, Hangzhou and Beijing. So, dominating the draught beer category could be a strategy for Tiger Beer to use.

THE FURTHER YOU GO, THE HARDER IT IS TO CONTROL THE BRAND

In countries where Tiger Beer is only exported to and does not have a local presence in terms of a branch office, the challenges that it faces are slightly different. In these markets, the biggest concern is how Tiger Beer can maintain consistent communications of its brand. It becomes more difficult to maintain consistency when you do not have your own people on the ground. It is already hard enough even with your own people, so you can imagine how much more difficult it becomes when you do not have your own people.

Tiger Beer's head office in Singapore will just have to work harder to make sure that each of these countries adheres to Tiger Beer's communications and corporate identity guidelines.

Tiger Beer seems to face bigger challenges in Asia as a result of its non-European heritage. Two of the biggest challenges that it faces are in persuading beer drinkers and trade partners to prefer the Tiger Beer brand, and in persuading consumers to pay more for the brand. The second challenge is not as serious because with some 30 breweries in 12 countries, Tiger Beer is quite well positioned and so transportation costs can be minimised. It does not mean that I am advocating a low price strategy but unlike in the United States or Europe, Tiger Beer does not have to sell at a premium in these Asian countries.

I suppose Tiger Beer will just have to narrow its focus even more and try very hard to drive home the point that it has won so many gold medals in international beer competitions held in Western countries. This takes time, and requires focus and consistency. Tiger Beer cannot afford to waver even a little. Its latest campaign "Unravel The Secret", which focused attention on Tiger Beer's award winning ways, is great. Future campaigns should continue to revolve around this powerful differentiator. It requires sacrifice. That means no more Jessica Alba-style TV commercials. Anything and everything that Tiger Beer advertises in Asia must communicate that it is a gold medal winning beer. Some people may find this a bit constraining but there is no other way around it. You can be as creative as you want with your brand communications but that creativity had better communicate your unique selling proposition consistently or you will have a hard time convincing people to buy your brand.

EASY COME, EASY GO

Tiger Beer believes that when it comes to marketing its beer, having local market knowledge is crucial as every market has its own quirks and peculiarities that might not be apparent to a foreigner. As such, Tiger Beer tries to populate its local marketing team with as many locals as possible. And because beer is a fun lifestyle product, it is never hard to attract good people to work for a beer company.

According to Tiger Beer, however, it is not easy to keep these people. Tiger Beer believes in training its people well and giving them the opportunity to plan and execute marketing strategies in the local markets. What this means is that Tiger Beer people become quite marketable and as a result, they get poached by other companies, not necessarily other beer companies but companies from industries such as banking, telecoms and electronics.

The other problem is that beer is basically a nocturnal product. Unless you are a serious alcoholic, you will not be drinking beer during the day. So, most of the marketing activities and promotions take place at night at entertainment spots like night clubs, karaoke lounges, bars and discos. This is fun for the Tiger Beer people but too much of that kind of nightlife will cause people to burn out easily. That is a big problem facing Tiger Beer. Well, there is nothing much that can be done about that; it's just the nature of the job. The good thing is, replacements are usually not hard to come by.

THE WORLD IS GETTING DARKER

Tiger Beer expects more and more countries around the world to go dark and ban alcohol advertising. That would present a huge problem for a brand like Tiger Beer in most countries as beer is a commodity that is very dependent on advertising as a brand-building tool. Any ban on advertising would hurt Tiger Beer's efforts. When a country goes dark, the incumbent brand will usually rejoice because no advertising means it would be difficult for challengers like Tiger Beer to launch an attack on them—it is not impossible but extremely difficult. In Tiger Beer's Dark Markets, like Vietnam for instance, it has had to use other methods to reach out to its customers. These methods could include more innovative point-of-purchase displays, sponsorships of events or other guerilla marketing tactics.

THE STORY OF VIETNAM

It is easy to understand why some brands don't venture out of their home market even after many successful decades. Taking a brand out of its comfort zone is a hard thing to do. It was no different for Tiger Beer, as it meant venturing outside its circle of competence, so to speak.

But Tiger Beer had no choice—Singapore is just too small. Staying put would mean staying small and eventually stagnate. So, it had to push the brand beyond the narrow confines of the island republic. The Tiger needed to be let out of its cage at some point in time. If you ask the people at Asia Pacific Breweries (APB) whether the process of internationalisation was difficult, the pioneers involved will tell you that it was not only difficult but the odds they faced were at times almost insurmountable. Take Vietnam, where Tiger Beer had to cope with fierce (and occasionally weird) problems when they were trying to establish a foothold in the northern region in 1994.

Bear in mind that Vietnam today is very different from what it was in 1994. Today, it is a rapidly modernising and industrialising nation. Its 84 million strong population makes it the 13th most populated country in the world. In fact, Goldman Sachs has classified Vietnam as one of the Next 11 (or N-11) countries in 2005, an N-11 country being one that has promising outlooks for investments and future growth.[1] As you can see from the table opposite, Vietnam's economy grew rapidly at an average of 7.4 per cent between 2000 and 2005, faster than the other N-11 countries, and it also has the highest trade openness at 134.2 per cent. Looks like Vietnam is a good market to venture into today. However, the story was a very different one back then.

In 1994, Tiger Beer had already established itself in the south, in Ho Chi Minh City, with a brewery near by. APB was eyeing Hanoi in the more conservative north as its next centre of operations. It set up a small representative office there, and with a three-man staff— all locals—it began talks with potential partners. The excitement of a joint venture was palpable for both parties. And then a spanner fell into the works. Deep into negotiations, APB realised that the local partners were only interested in the internationally renowned Heineken, which APB also brews. APB, of course, wanted the new brewery to produce and distribute its homegrown Tiger Beer.

SO, WHAT DID TIGER BEER DO?

Despite the setback, APB decided not to put its expansion on hold but to push resolutely into the north alone. First, it despatched a young manager from Singapore to head the Hanoi office. This

1. Global Economics Paper No. 147 – Jim O'Neill, Sun Bae Kim and Jim Buchanan, 2005.

SNAPSHOT OF N-11 COUNTRIES

Country	Population (million)	GDP (US$ billion)	2000 – 2005 Average GDP Growth Rate (%)	GDP Per Capita (US$)	Trade Openness (% GDP)	Urbanisation (% Total)	Foreign Direct Investment (% GDP)
Bangladesh	144	61	5.6	400	36.7	25.0	0.8
Egypt	78	89	4.0	1,265	53.6	42.3	4.6
Indonesia	242	281	4.8	1,283	51.0	47.9	1.2
Iran	68	192	5.7	2,767	51.7	68.1	0.3
Korea	49	788	5.2	16,308	68.6	80.8	0.6
Mexico	106	768	2.7	7,298	57.5	76.0	2.2
Nigeria	129	99	5.6	678	71.9	48.3	3.0
Pakistan	162	111	5.0	728	37.2	34.8	1.0
Philippines	88	98	4.7	1,168	90.1	62.6	0.5
Turkey	70	362	5.0	5,062	51.9	67.3	1.3
Vietnam	84	51	7.4	618	134.2	26.7	3.6

Source: IMF, World Bank, UN and GS calculations

manager has grown with the company and today helms the entire export markets business. In Tiger Beer parlance, an export market is defined as a market that it does not have a brewery in. An export market is by nature a harder one to penetrate due to the handicap of not having a local brewery.

One problem the manager faced was that of language. He didn't speak Vietnamese but being young, idealistic and not fully aware of the difficulties that awaited him in Hanoi, he took the job anyway. At the airport, he was shocked to learn that there was no direct road to the Sofitel Metropole Hotel where he was to stay. With a non-English speaking driver, he was taken on a 2-hour long, circuitous route through many villages to get to the city. (Today, with a modern highway, it takes the visitor a mere 20 minutes. Then, it also took Tiger Beer's delivery trucks three days and three nights of non-stop driving—plus two drivers—to make the trip north from Ho Chi Minh City, just so the brew got to the consumer fresh!). But the language barrier was a small problem compared to what he was about to face.

THE CHALLENGES, PART 1
MANAGING A LOCAL SALES TEAM

The first step for Tiger Beer was to put in place an effective sales team. The Hanoi office needed ten people to begin with. That didn't turn out to be as big a challenge as Tiger Beer thought as there were many bright, young tertiary educated Vietnamese eager to work for a foreign company; in those days, it was quite a novelty to work for such companies. Some of the staff spoke English, others didn't, but that was manageable.

The real challenge was in striking a balance between Tiger Beer's way of doing things and letting the local team use its knowledge of the local market to formulate tactics that were workable. As the then manager sees it today, the biggest mistake that any foreign company can make in Vietnam is to underestimate the intelligence and drive of the local people. Tiger Beer wouldn't have been as successful in Vietnam if it didn't tap into the talent and local market knowledge of its staff. Managing a local team in a culturally different foreign market was something that he had to learn on the job. He had to think on his feet. He had to improvise. He had to do an environmental scan of what he had on hand, what he had to work with, and make the best of the situation.

GETTING INTO THE PSYCHE OF THE RETAILERS
AND CONSUMERS

At that time, Tiger Beer had no distribution channel to speak of in Hanoi. Tiger Beer had to readjust its way of thinking. In the more developed markets, it could appoint distributors to get the beer to restaurants, hawker centres, supermarkets and bars. However, in Hanoi, where the Tiger Beer brand was unknown and the market not as sophisticated, it had to start right at the bottom and build up a distribution channel one coffee shop at a time.

And it is here that Tiger Beer spotted a weakness in the local market that it could exploit. At that time, most suppliers in Hanoi were state-owned companies governed by red tape. If you wanted to sell something, you would have to plead with the companies to let you sell their goods. Needless to say, the service level that retailers received from their suppliers was almost non-existent.

Tiger Beer therefore put in place a clever strategy to woo the eating outlets and shops where beer was sold. It would send a salesperson to visit these places and chat with the owner; it would be just small talk. That personal outreach was appreciated because suppliers NEVER sent their people to talk to shop owners. Naturally, shop owners sat up and took notice of Tiger Beer. After an hour or two, the Tiger Beer representative would take out two bottles of Tiger Beer from his backpack, put it on the counter and ask the shop owner to try out this brand of beer from Singapore.

And because the shop owner was impressed with the politeness and eloquence of the salesperson, he would very often accept the two bottles. Then the salesperson would take his leave. Tiger Beer would later send two other people to the shop, at separate times, to order a bottle of the brew. The shop owner would be pleasantly surprised. Now, this may seem like an old sales trick but it worked for Tiger Beer. Shops and eating outlets started buying and promoting the brew to their customers, partly because they were impressed with the service level and partly because they thought the brand would sell.

It was hard work but the people in the Hanoi office knew there was no short cut to success. They had to build up the brand outlet by outlet, one bottle at a time. But the hard work paid off. Within three months, Tiger Beer became the best selling beer in Hanoi ... and this was when the real trouble began.

THE CHALLENGES, PART 2
TROUBLE WITH THE AUTHORITIES

Tiger Beer's quick success raised the ire of its competitors. Naturally they got jealous and began to block this young upstart from making further inroads into the Hanoi market. That is actually the right thing to do. As any good business school will teach you, the newcomer's job is to attack the incumbent and the incumbent's job is to block the newcomer. Nothing unusual about that. In fact, it was to be expected.

What Tiger Beer did not expect, however, was how quickly and aggressively its competitors began to block its marketing efforts. Being a small start-up in that market meant Tiger Beer had to put up with fierce resistance from more established players. Also, some of Tiger Beer's competitors might even have complained to the authorities that its salespeople were gangsters, as over a period of a few months, the police were detaining its sales staff for questioning. Naturally, the police must investigate when there are complaints of this nature because it is their job to protect public interest.

The manager had to think fast. He knew his team was not doing anything wrong and so felt the best way was to carry on with their work in a friendly and transparent manner, and ride out the storm. He approached the episode calmly and cooperated with the authorities. His persistence paid off and after a few months, his team was cleared of any wrongdoing. Nonetheless, it was still a stressful time for everyone. The experience was bewildering, to say the least, although he can now look back and laugh at this colourful moment in the brand's history. Litlle did he know, however, that there was an even bigger problem looming up— one that was potentially more damaging.

TROUBLE IN THE PRESS

Around the same time, several newspapers in Hanoi also published negative stories about Tiger Beer, labelling its salespeople as gangsters. The reports puzzled Tiger Beer's distributors and retailers, as their relationship with Tiger Beer had always been good. Again, the manager responded to the situation calmly although the urge 'to do something' was great. And once again, his patience paid off.

Deciding that the stories about Tiger Beer were one-sided, the *Vietnam Economic Times* ran a double-page spread allowing Tiger Beer and its main competitor to each tell their side of the story, and let readers decide for themselves the truth of the allegations. This put a close to the matter and Tiger Beer emerged from the ordeal a stronger brand than ever.

Brand It Like
Tiger Beer

7

For those who want to build a strong brand, there are some very important lessons that can be learnt from Tiger Beer. Tiger Beer did not get to where it is by chance. Although it was not insusceptible to mistakes, it has done more things right than wrong. Otherwise, it would not have grown to become the iconic Singapore brand that it is today. So, what are the important lessons that we can learn from this brand's journey over the past 75 years?

BRANDS ARE BUILT ON VISION, NOT OPPORTUNITIES

That is right—to build a brand, you need a vision. That is what separates a brand from a business. A business will just chase any market opportunities that it can find. A business would probably want to own 5 per cent of ten markets instead of 50 per cent of one market. That is the typical mentality of many Singapore companies that I have met and continue to meet because they think this approach is easier and less risky. But these businesses do not understand a simple mathematical equation. When you try to own 5 per cent of ten markets, you are actually fighting the marketing war on ten different fronts with ten different sets of competitors. That is tough. But if you build up strength in one market and become big before you try to venture into another market, that makes things a little easier. Toyota did that. Only after the Corolla became the best selling car in the world (yes, the world) did it try to venture into the luxury car market with Lexus. After Lexus became No.1 in the United States, it launched a new brand, Scion, for the youth market.

A brand, on the other hand, is driven by a vision. A brand is willing to give up nine out of ten markets that it could have chased just so that it can dominate one. Starbucks gave up everything that it could have served so that it could dominate the gourmet coffee market. Before Starbucks came along, cafes served everything—coffee, tea, milkshakes, sandwiches, pasta, eggs, steak, chicken, salads, burgers, and so on. Starbucks gave up everything else to become No. 1 in gourmet coffee. A brand would rather have 50 per cent of one market than 5 per cent of ten markets.

If Fraser and Neave had been driven by opportunities rather than vision in 1932, it might have decided that it made better sense to just brew and sell several established European brands than try to build a Singapore beer brand. Fortunately for us, Fraser and Neave was either very visionary or completely unaware of the difficulties of building a beer brand that is Singaporean in origin, or both. Tiger Beer does not have 50 per cent of the world beer market yet but in some of the countries, such as Singapore, Malaysia, Thailand and Vietnam, it is big and dominant. Furthermore, Tiger Beer dominates the category called *exotic Asian beer* because it was willing to sacrifice many things that it could have done just to become this. When this category grows, Tiger Beer will grow along with it.

You need a bold vision to build a brand and the vision of Tiger Beer has never been anything less than bold. Right from day one, it wanted to become the "World Acclaimed" Asian beer. That was why it entered the brew into its first international beer competition in 1939, just seven years after the brand was born. And Tiger Beer won too—a bronze medal. Not bad at all for a young debutante. Tiger Beer continues to be driven by its vision. It has never wavered. It is relentless in its focus, which is very heartening for me personally because many Singapore companies are not very focused; they try to do too many things and be too many things. One of the reasons why Tiger Beer never wavered is because it has a clear

vision, and this vision focused the brand and never let it wander off the straight and narrow.

BRAND BUILDING NEEDS MONEY

Even the most brilliant branding strategy in the world will be for nothing if you are under capitalised. If you do not have enough money, things may not happen. When I was branding manager at International Enterprise Singapore, I was introduced to the agency's 3C framework for helping Singapore companies succeed in international markets—Competency, Connections and Capital. That's right. Money is what makes the business world go round.

However, many brands do not make it, not because the company does not have enough money, but because the company does not have enough faith in the concept to pump in enough money for the new brand to have a chance at success. Fortunately, Fraser and Neave saw enough potential in this new business to pump in sufficient money for the brand to take off.

In many companies, management tries to hedge their bets by portioning out money for new projects or brands equally. They see this as spreading the risks but most companies are not big enough—like General Electric or Hewlett Packard or IBM or 3M or Intel—to do that. You have to make carefully considered decisions and then place your bets on one or two things that you think can reap the biggest rewards. It is the 80/20 rule all over again. Twenty per cent of what you do will give you 80 per cent of the revenue. The trick is to find that 20 per cent to pour your resources into. Fraser and Neave did all the right things when it came to putting enough money behind the Tiger Beer brand in terms of infrastructure, marketing and innovation. As a result, it has a winner today.

BRAND BUILDING TAKES TIME

Rome was not built in a day. Oak trees do not grow overnight. And brands take time to build. Brand building requires patience. I have seen brands go down the drain in as little as two years. From powerful, confident, money making machines, these brands suddenly find themselves so deep in debt and losses that they do not know what hit them. It all boils down to impatience. These brands try to force growth on to the brands. You can't do that.

Growing a brand is like growing a plant. It takes time. It takes patience. It requires consistent care and nurture. If you are an impatient person, you will use too much fertiliser and too much water, and ultimately kill the plant. A brand is the same. Growth comes from doing things right and doing the right things consistently over time. If you are impatient, you should not try to grow a plant or manage your brand because that impatience will kill both the plant and your brand. For this reason, Tiger Beer is very careful in its expansion plans. It could have easily picked up the pace but it chose to do the right thing. It would rather have careful and constant growth than rapid expansion that would stress the brand to breaking point. That is a lesson that we can all learn from Tiger Beer.

THE MAIN THING IS TO KEEP THE MAIN THING, THE MAIN THING

One of the things that most companies do when they get to be moderately successful is that they take their eyes off the ball. They forget what made them successful in the first place. That is just human nature. When you do that, your core business gets neglected and over time it allows your competitors to overtake you. That is why companies go through a very predictable cycle of expansion and consolidation because when they become successful, they will try to get into all kinds of unrelated businesses. Then they bomb and have to scramble to offload their non-core businesses, usually at a huge loss. If they are lucky, they will get the core business going again, but over time they forget and start to make the same mistakes again. You need to keep the main thing the main thing. Do not digress. If you do, it will lead you to your destruction.

When Mercedes-Benz bought Chrysler, I said to anyone who cared to listen that the merger would fail, that it would damage Mercedes-Benz and do no good to Chrysler. Why? On paper, it looked like a fantastic marriage. Mercedes-Benz would gain a sister company that would allow it to expand into the mass market and Chrysler would get access to Mercedes-Benz's highly vaunted engineering capabilities. That was wishful thinking. The merger would only drag Mercedes-Benz down in terms of quality (Mercedes-Benz quality did suffer a big drop during this time) and it would slow Chrysler down. Chrysler is known for its ability to bring stunning concept cars into production in record time, usually less than three years, whereas other companies take four to six years. But having to conform to Mercedes-Benz's engineering practice meant slowing down this process and dampening Chrysler's creativity. At the time I was writing this book, the Daimler Chrysler divorce happened. Chrysler was sold off to private equity firm Cerberus for US$7.4 billion. That may sound like a lot of money but Chrysler was bought for around US$35 billion! This happened because Mercedes-Benz did not keep the main thing the main thing. The main thing is? Luxury cars ... cars that exude uncompromising German engineering and oodles of prestige.

Tiger Beer has so far managed to avoid this trap although it did dabble briefly into line extensions with the Tiger Stout and Tiger Extra Stout, which it later discontinued to remain focused on the main thing—Tiger Beer. The task of building the stout market was handed over to Archipelago Brewery Company (which Tiger Beer's parent company Malayan Breweries had bought over) and a new brand was created—ABC Stout. Companies can learn a very important lesson from this. Mercedes-Benz could have learnt an important lesson from this, a lesson that would have saved them tens of billions of dollars. Tiger Beer has so far been extremely focused on what the brand stands for and what it is all about. It has not forgotten what it is that made it famous. Instead, it is looking to take this success formula further.

BRANDS MUST HAVE QUALITY AT LEAST AS GOOD AS THE COMPETITION'S

That is right. Quality is no longer a differentiator but it is something that even people buying the cheapest entry level products will expect. Just because they buy a cheap, entry level television set from China does not mean that they are fine with the picture being greenish. They expect the picture to be clear. The quality of your television must be at least as good as the other televisions being sold in the market or nobody will buy from you.

Tiger Beer understands this very well, which is why it benchmarks itself ceaselessly against other brands. It is also the reason why it works hard to make sure that its product quality remains consistently high. That is one of the reasons why it continues to

participate in international beer competitions even though it has won so many gold medals. Participating in these competitions keeps Tiger Beer on its toes because the feedback from the judges will tell Tiger Beer how its beer is faring against the other brands. If other brands have improved because they are using a new type of filtering process, for example, then Tiger Beer will have to improve. If it does not, it will be left behind eventually. No matter how strong your brand is, if your quality does not keep in line with that of your competitors', then your brand will be damaged.

The other lesson to learn is that the easier it is for your customers to switch brands, the more careful you have to be. Tiger Beer knows that well enough.

BRANDS CANNOT AVOID THE PROCESS OF GLOBALISATION

Tiger Beer could have easily remained in its home markets of Singapore and Malaysia, and be content with its small pond. After all, that is what a lot of Singapore companies do. Stay in one place and expand by getting into other types of businesses within Singapore. Tiger Beer realised a long time ago that the process of globalisation is inevitable and that it must expand into other markets and grow bigger so that it can stay alive. If it just remains in Singapore and Malaysia, it will eventually get run over by the big boys because size does matter.

Look around you. In every country that you look, the big global brands are taking over. Well, in most open markets anyway. In some countries, protectionist policies are still in place that allow uncompetitive local brands to survive. Not in Singapore. Anyone can come in to compete with Tiger Beer. The barriers to entry are low. The only way for Tiger Beer to compete is by becoming a big brand itself. And unlike other indigenous brands like Asahi and Kirin of Japan, Tsingtao of China, and San Miguel of the Philippines, Tiger Beer does not have a big local market. So, it needs to go global and expand its footprint. As the Borgs in Star Trek would say: "Resistance is futile."

BRANDS MUST INVEST IN THE RIGHT PEOPLE

One of the things that Tiger Beer has on the top of its priority list is that it must find the right kind of people who believe in the brand and will do the right thing so that the brand is enhanced through their actions. James Wong, General Manager of Tiger Export International, was on a discussion panel at the International Enterprise Forum 2007 on "Export Branding". I happened to chair that panel discussion. I asked James what he thought was the most important factor that accounted for Tiger Beer's international success, and he repeated several times that it is the people. He advised the companies that were present at the forum to focus on their people because a brand is ultimately about the collective skills and convictions of its people.

I agree. When you are small, you can do everything on your own but in order for a brand to grow, it must have the right people. Without people, it is impossible to scale up a business for international expansion. A chain is as strong as its weakest link and a brand is only as strong as the people behind it. So, you need to invest in the right people. You get the wrong people and they would probably do more harm than good. And after getting the right people, you still need to train them, motivate them, monitor them and reward them properly.

8

What Next?

The future looks bright for Tiger Beer. I'm not saying

this because Tiger Beer has thrived against all odds and become a successful brand in both its Asian and Western markets. I'm not saying this because Tiger Beer seemed to have gotten away with murder in adopting two different brand positions—one for Asia and one for the West.

I am saying this because on a corporate level, Tiger Beer adopts an underdog mentality. The people at Tiger Beer talk a lot about how Tiger Beer is handicapped by being a Singaporean product, and so they cannot afford to get cocky. They talk about needing constant external validation of the brand in order to survive. That kind of thinking keeps Tiger Beer on its toes and is an effective guard against complacency. I like what I hear because these people remind me of Andy Grove, the legendary co-founder of Intel. Andy Grove is paranoid. Andy Grove wrote a book called *Only The Paranoid Survive*. Despite Intel's size and success, with a market share of over 80 per cent, Intel remained paranoid. Intel kept challenging itself. It kept pushing itself. You can say Intel's biggest enemy is ... Intel!

The same kind of attitude prevails at Tiger Beer. Despite its hard earned success, Tiger Beer is not resting on its laurels. The attitude at Tiger Beer is this: You are only as good as what you do next. Tiger Beer knows that all those gold medals and market success mean nothing if it does not constantly challenge itself to do better. The people are always on their toes. They will continue to push the performance envelope in terms of marketing and product quality. I will not say that Tiger Beer is as paranoid as Intel was when Andy Grove was at the helm, but enough of that quality exists in Tiger Beer to make sure it does not get complacent and slip.

I am also writing this down so that any Tiger Beer people—current and future—reading this will be reminded of how important it is to constantly push the brand higher and higher.

The other thing that makes me most confident about Tiger Beer is this. The folks at Tiger Beer may not be aware of it but they are doing many of the things that a brand should do in order to become strong brands. They are practising all the rules of branding—ten of them—that I strongly believe in. Here are the ten rules that I think Tiger Beer is playing closely by which will augur well for its future.

RULE NO. 1 — PERCEPTION IS REALITY

Everyone I speak to at Tiger Beer seems acutely aware that the one thing that makes a difference in all their marketing efforts is perception. Perception is reality. As far as customers are concerned, what they perceive to be true is the truth. They do not really care about what the company says. All they care about is what they perceive. Branding is a game that takes place in the mind. The mind is where the battle of branding is won or lost. Read the sentence below.

TIGERISNOWHERE

What does it say? Some of you would see this as 'Tiger Is Nowhere'. And some of you would see this as 'Tiger Is Now Here'. It does not matter what I say this sentence is. If you perceive the sentence as one way, that is the way it is. If you perceive the sentence as another way, then that is the way it is going to be. All that matters is how you perceive the sentence.

It is the same in branding. Yes, quality and service are important but these are factors that are expected of every brand, even the ones that are supposedly entry level. What makes the difference is how people see the brand. If they see Tiger Beer as good, then it is good. If they see it as no good, then it is no good.

That is why Tiger Beer tracks customer perceptions relentlessly using more than one independent (and reputable, of course) brand research agencies. Tiger Beer has shown me chart after chart after chart of the results of its perception tracking. I cannot reproduce the charts here but take my word for it—Tiger Beer knows exactly how the brand is perceived in any given period of time. It knows how a particular marketing programme, TV commercial or press release is affecting customer perception of the brand. Tiger Beer tracks this brand perception relentlessly so that it can immediately fix anything that is causing perception of the brand to deteriorate before it becomes impossible to fix it.

RULE NO. 2 — IT IS BETTER TO BE FIRST

The brands that make it big are usually the brands that got into the market first. However, there are so many first mover failures. How do you explain that? Branding is something that takes place in the mind. Products are made in factories. Beer is brewed in breweries. But brands are created in the mind. Being first in the market is not the be all and end all. Being first in the market just gives you the licence to establish your brand in the mind before anyone else does. If you do not exploit that licence, then that's too bad for you.

Because Tiger Beer is not the first beer brand in the world, it is at a disadvantage. That is why it tries to do things that are a first in the beer industry in order to establish the brand in the mind. The way Tiger Beer uses unconventional marketing platforms such as Tiger FC, Tiger Translate and TigerLIVE is inspiring because these are firsts that can generate a positive perception of the Tiger Beer brand.

People also tend to think that the first brand is the best brand. The first brand has heritage and originality on its side. But heritage does not help much if you are a technology company. Plus, claiming to be the original will probably be detrimental to the brand as people may think that it is an outdated dinosaur. On the other hand, being the first brand or the original brand helps in other categories like beverage (Coke: The Real Thing); jeans (Levi's: The Original Jeans); and traditional Chinese medicine (Eu Yan Sang). Since Tiger Beer cannot help the fact that it is not first in most markets, it tries to invent new things that it can be first in.

RULE NO. 3 — CREATE A NEW CATEGORY

Tiger Beer knows that in many markets, it is not the first brand and so it created new categories that it can be first in. Creating a new category and then promoting that category was what built some of the world's best brands. Starbucks created a new category called *gourmet coffee* and promoted that category aggressively to become the biggest coffee chain in the world. The Body Shop created a new category called *environmentally friendly cosmetics* and promoted that category aggressively to become a global leader. Red Bull created a new category called *energy drink* and promoted that category aggressively to become the No. 1 energy drink brand in the world and one of the Top 10 beverage brands in the lucrative United States market.

So, what new category did Tiger Beer pioneer? *Asia's world acclaimed lager beer.* Asia is not known for beer but here is a beer from Asia that has won over 40 international awards in the most prestigious beer competitions. No other Asian beer comes close. In fact, very few Western beers come close. That is a great thing. It is a fantastic new category—an Asian beer that could mix with the best of the West. And Tiger Beer is re-focusing its efforts on promoting this category with its latest packaging design that gives more prominence to the medals and the latest TV commercial that revolves entirely around Tiger Beer's award winning heritage.

I did say in the first sentence of this section that Tiger Beer created new categories. That is not a typing error. Most successful brands pioneer ONE category and make use of that category to make them famous. However, you are well aware by now that Tiger Beer is in a unique position because of the peculiarities of the Asian and Western markets. In Asia, being Asian is no big deal. It is just like going to India to eat Indian food. To the folks in India, it is just food! But in Latin America, Indian food could be seen as somewhat exotic. In the West, being Asian helps create a Far East mystique that Tiger Beer could exploit. Hence, Tiger Beer needed two categories—one Western, one Asian.

In Asia, the category is *Asia's world acclaimed lager beer*. In the West, Tiger Beer is the *exotic beer from the Far East*. Well, it has worked so far because Tiger Beer is very careful to maintain its consistency in these two key geographic markets. It did not allow the Western brand strategy to contaminate its Asian brand strategy and vice versa.

RULE NO. 4 — THE POWER OF FOCUS

I love this rule! It has many a time given me an excuse to avoid doing a lot of the things that I do not like doing. When you focus, you become good at what you do. People also think you are good at what you do. This was what happened to Tiger Beer.

Tiger Beer has been one of the most focused beer brands in the world for the last 75 years. Tiger Beer is a lager beer. Tiger Beer comes in an amber coloured glass bottle. Canned beer was added to meet market demand but that is fine since everyone else was doing it too. However, Tiger Beer has been resolutely focused on being the best lager beer in the world. This focus made Tiger Beer good. Just look at how many medals Tiger Beer has won and compare that to highly diversified beer brands like Miller or Budweiser.

The other thing is, the focus makes people think that Tiger Beer is good. I know a lot of Tiger Beer drinkers. I had this theory that they only drank Tiger Beer because it was the cheapest beer in Singapore. So, I offered to buy other brands of beer for these friends of mine. I tried with Heineken, I tried with Tuborg, I tried with Beck's, and many others. To my surprise, these people insisted only on Tiger Beer. They must have thought that Tiger Beer was the best! Because if the only reason for buying the brand was because it was cheap, then they would have jumped at my offer to buy other pricier brands.

One more thing, Tiger Beer has rarely used line extensions. It has one that is called Tiger Crystal, which it exports to the China market, but even with this it is treading carefully to make sure that the brand's strong focus is not diluted.

RULE NO. 5 — DIFFERENTIATE THE BRAND

With so many beer brands in the world, it is easy to get your product lost on a supermarket shelf. Tiger Beer understands this only too well. That is why it tries to differentiate its brand as much as it can. Differentiation is necessary to build a strong brand. But I always tell people that you need to be different but not to be different for the sake of being different. Be different with a great idea, not a stupid one. And that point of differentiation must be relevant, as well as desirable and defensible, for customers.

We have already seen how Tiger Beer differentiated itself from other Asian beers by being the one that is "world acclaimed". That is actually one of the 13 differentiation strategies that my firm uses for client branding projects. What Tiger Beer is doing here is using a differentiation strategy we call Preference. By being "world acclaimed", by winning all those medals at international competitions, Tiger Beer is showing customers that it is preferred by beer experts. It is. After all, the people who awarded Tiger Beer those medals over the past seven and a half decades are the world's foremost experts on beer. So, if beer experts prefer Tiger Beer, why wouldn't you? Again, this is the strategy for Asian markets.

Tiger Beer also differentiates itself from Western beers by being the "exotic Asian beer". That is another differentiation strategy we call Heritage. In a world full of Western beers, Tiger Beer stands out by playing up its Asian heritage. More than the Asian heritage, it plays up the association between Asian and exotic. This is the strategy for the West.

But beyond that, Tiger Beer also tries to differentiate the actual product through its packaging. A bottled Tiger Beer is always in that now famous amber coloured bottle. It differentiates Tiger Beer from leading European brands like Heineken, Carlsberg and Beck's, which are all in green bottles. The canned Tiger Beer comes in blue cans. Not just any blue but an electric blue that immediately makes it stand out among a sea of green cans. In fact, I think the blue can is even more effective in differentiating Tiger Beer visually than the amber bottle because as far as I know, nobody uses blue.

Tiger Beer's current look is fresh and spirited. A prominent brand element is the Tiger shield, with the brew's medal awards stamped on it.

RULE NO. 6 — USE PUBLIC RELATIONS TO BUILD THE BRAND

Early on, I said that advertising is the traditional way of building up a beer brand, any beer. Tiger Beer, however, has moved away from that path. Tiger Beer told me that it wants to use public relations more than ever in its brand building efforts. It points out, and correctly so, that public relations has more credibility than advertising. Advertising is what you say about yourself, and what you say about yourself is often perceived as biased, and so it is not very believable.

Public relations is what the media say about you and since the media is a third party, it is perceived as neutral and hence more credible. However, this publicity is not easy to achieve since the media can talk about a thousand and one things, so you need to give them a great reason to talk about your brand. Tiger Beer has found that great reason. By supporting upcoming Asian artists, musicians and movie makers through its Tiger Translate platform and bringing the best of Asia to the West, Tiger Beer has generated plenty of media interest. I was told that Tiger Beer managed to

At TigerLIVE in St James Power Station, visitors learn about the fine art of tapping and serving super cold beer in Tiger Super Cold, one of eight specially created interactive experiences.

get millions of dollars worth of publicity through this platform. The TigerLIVE display at the St James Power Station also generated a lot of publicity for the brand.

Now that Tiger Beer has tasted the power of public relations, it will continue to generate events and platforms that will be newsworthy enough for the media to talk about. The idea behind public relations is not to promote the brand but to promote something else that is new and exciting. The brand is just there for the ride. By creating all these new platforms, Tiger Beer has got the media interested. Tiger Beer just happened to be there for the ride. The focus was the event. The beneficiary? Why, Tiger Beer, of course.

RULE NO. 7 — HAVE A GREAT NAME

Well, the name 'Tiger' can't be changed now but I think the name works. A name needs to be short, unique, easy to pronounce, memorable and work in the English language. 'Tiger' is a short word (two syllables) and most of the world's greatest brands have names with two syllables. But while 'Tiger' is not a unique word, it is unique to Tiger Beer in its category. No other beer has a similar sounding name. It is easy to pronounce; how many people cannot pronounce 'Tiger'? It is memorable because it is quite different from the other beer brands. And it works in English since it is an English word. Names do not have to be English; they just need to work in the English language. 'Nokia' is not an English word but it can still be easily pronounced in English.

RULE NO. 8 — THE POWER OF CONSISTENCY

This is something that Tiger Beer knows better than most. Brand building is not an exciting game as many people might think. Brand building is the world's most boring game because you need absolute consistency. You need to do the same thing day in day out with little or no variation. You need to be absolutely consistent—from your brand strategy and product quality to your brand communications, and everything in between. Inconsistency will lead to a brand with multiple personalities and nobody likes to hang around a schizophrenic brand. Tiger Beer works hard to maintain consistency in every aspect of the brand. Just take a look at how the Tiger Beer logo and packaging have evolved over the years. The look and feel have been updated on a regular basis but you can still tell that it is Tiger Beer. That is consistency.

RULE NO. 9 — MAKE ENEMIES, NOT FRIENDS

If you want to build a strong brand, you have to make some enemies. Brands need a reason to live. Having an enemy to fight gives your brand a reason to exist. Pepsi has a reason to exist because it has an enemy to fight—Coca-Cola. Burger King has a reason to exist because it has an enemy to fight—McDonald's.

But the enemy may not necessarily be another brand. It could be a cause or an existing category. For example, when the electric typewriter came along, Brother used the new category to go against the existing category (mechanical typewriter) and became a big brand. Then the word processor came along and Wang used that new category to go against the electric typewriter. The personal computer then made the electric typewriter obsolete.

So, another thing to consider is that Tiger Beer's enemies might not be other beer brands. They could include other alcoholic beverages like whisky, brandy, wine, and so on. Tiger Beer could use its category *world acclaimed Asian lager beer* as a weapon to go against the current world order. Making enemies is something that Tiger Beer is not yet doing but this is something that it could do to make the brand more edgy and visible.

RULE NO. 10 — LAUNCH A SECOND BRAND

Every brand will grow to a stage where it needs to launch new products. That is when it must decide whether to use the existing brand's name on the new product or launch a new brand. My preferred strategy is to launch a new brand for a new product because that will allow the existing brand to maintain its focus and it will free the new product from any baggage that might come as a result of being linked to an existing brand.

For example, Kodak is a brand that is known for photographic film. Kodak also (surprise! surprise!) invented digital photography in 1976. But is Kodak the leading digital camera today? No. Why? Because the wrong brand was used on the camera. It is for the same reason that Toyota launched Lexus when it wanted to enter the luxury car market in 1989. It then launched Scion to enter the youth market several years ago.

Tiger Beer needs to bear this in mind. Once Tiger Beer is known for something, it should stick with it. Any new product should carry a different brand rather than a line extension of the Tiger Beer brand. So far, Tiger Beer does not have any plans to launch new brands because Tiger Beer is part of Asia Pacific Breweries (APB). It is APB's flagship brand, no doubt, but the parent company also owns a portfolio of other alcoholic beverage brands. Among Tiger Beer's siblings are ABC Extra Stout, Baron's Strong Brew, Anchor Beer and Heineken.

- ABC Extra Stout

  APB's proprietary ABC Extra Stout is designed to reflect its core drinker's values and self-image, which the company has defined as determined, confident and successful. ABC Extra Stout drinkers are characterised as knowing what they want and willing to go the extra mile to get it. They want the best and do not settle for anything less. Appreciated for its full-bodied and robust taste, ABC Extra Stout is the leading premium stout in Cambodia.

• Baron's Strong Brew

Launched in Singapore in 1997, Baron's Strong Brew is European to the last drop. Traditionally blended from the finest European hops and malt for a strong smooth taste, Baron's delivers a message of solid European heritage. Its authenticity has translated into a strong presence in the high alcohol beer category. Baron's packaging is distinctive in design, reflecting its premium image and quality.

• Anchor Beer

Anchor Beer was first brewed in Singapore over 70 years ago using German technology and brew masters. Anchor's value-for-money positioning and its refreshing and signature crisp taste have clearly struck a chord with drinkers in over ten countries in Asia.

• Heineken

Heineken is embraced by drinkers in over 170 countries, and possesses the widest international presence of any international beer brand. It is distinctive in a green bottle and its exclusive image finds rapport with sophisticated young adult consumers who enjoy cutting edge music experiences and premier sporting events. Heineken is not a proprietary brand but it is one of the beers that APB brews. Heineken is a shareholder of APB after all.

So, APB actually has the market covered with its five brands. Heineken is the premium European brand to compete with premium European brands like Carlsberg and Beck's. ABC Extra Stout takes care of the stout market to compete with the likes of Guinness Stout. Baron's Strong Brew is the high alcohol content beer and takes care of that specialised segment of the market. Anchor Beer is the entry level brand that takes care of the budget category of the beer market. Tiger Beer, of course, is the world acclaimed exotic Asian beer.

With all these brands occupying different segments of the market, there is actually very little room for Tiger Beer to launch new brands. The last thing that Tiger Beer wants to do is to run into its siblings. It would be disastrous. It was what ruined the General Motors brand.

Many decades ago, under the leadership of the legendary Alfred P Sloan, General Motors had a very clear brand strategy. It owned a portfolio of brands, just like APB now owns several brands. Its brands—Chevrolet (US$450–US$600), Pontiac, Oldsmobile, Buick and Cadillac (over US$2,500)—were clearly segmented by price. After Sloan passed on, General Motors took its eyes off the ball and allowed its brand strategy to run wild. So, Chevrolet started moving up-market and Cadillac started moving down-market. All of its brands started running into each other's path, and that confused the market and damaged the General Motors brand. General Motors began to lose market share steadily in its home market of the United States. And it lost its position as the No. 1 car manufacturer in the world to Toyota.

APB has obviously learnt the lesson of General Motors even though General Motors has refused to learn it. As a result, Tiger Beer is very clear in the segmentation of its brands. However, there are still opportunities for Tiger Beer to launch new brands to tap into categories that APB currently has no brand representation. For example, light beer, ice beer and draught beer. However, Tiger Beer would need to have new brands for these new categories should it decide to enter them.

For the time being, though, Tiger Beer is focused on building its Tiger Beer brand. But if it continues to do the right things, it would someday grow to the point where it would need to consider launching new brands in order to continue its growth. There are two ways for a company to grow. The specialist way is to take one product (or service) and then expand it to as many countries as it can. The generalist way is to stay in one market and launch line extensions and sell more products under the same brand. The Tiger Beer way is the specialist way. It takes one product and expands it to many markets.

But what happens when Tiger Beer is eventually sold in every market that it can be sold in and there is no more room for growth? This is the law of diminishing returns that economists talk about—the closer you are to 100 per cent, the harder it is to make gains. So, Tiger Beer may one day get to the point where incremental market share would be too expensive to gain and not be worth it. When that happens, Tiger Beer might need to launch new brands into new categories in order to maintain its growth trajectory. But for now, the Tiger Beer brand still has a lot of room for growth.

A NEW LANDMARK IN CHINA.

FROM NOW, OUR BREWERIES
IN SHANGHAI AND FUZHOU WILL BE BREWING TIGER BEER.

Tiger has been so popular in Shanghai, and Fuzhou, we've decided to brew it in both cities. Over 43 million people there will now experience more of the taste that's been winning the world over. Enjoyed in over 50 countries around the world, and winner of 30 international gold medals for quality, Tiger Beer is sure to make its mark on China's landscape.

GOOD AS GOLD AROUND THE WORLD ← Tiger

the last word

For those of you who were hoping to unravel the secrets of Tiger Beer's success, you might be a little bit disappointed to find that there is no magic formula that could be attributed to the brand's success. That's right; branding is not rocket science. The principles of branding are actually quite easy to understand but they are not easy to apply because they are applied by people. People get so distracted by all kinds of theories and data that their minds get paralysed and they cannot act decisively. Also, because the principles of branding are easy enough to understand, many people are skeptical. "Can it really be that simple?"

The answer is yes. As you can see from Tiger Beer's success, it did not become successful because of one magic formula that propelled it to the top of the world. It became successful by doing things right. Not just one thing but many little things that, when put together, created the brand. And it also took a lot of hard work from many different people who worked in Tiger Beer all over the world.

In the latest series of Tiger Beer TV commercials called "Unravel The Secret", you will hear the voice-over saying: "Only ten know the secret". Well, now you also know the secret of Tiger Beer's success. As long as Tiger Beer continues to do the right things consistently and play by the rules of branding, I see no reason why the brand will not continue its growth.

The brand is confident because it has overcome a lot of challenges in its journey. The brand has picked up a lot of expertise and experience along the way. It has also gathered some fans as well. I think this brand will continue to be one of Singapore's most iconic brands and one day, it may even be cited as a prime example of a Singapore brand that has put the nation on the map, just like the way Singapore Airlines is now mentioned.

Finally, I would like to salute the men and women of Tiger Beer, both past, present and future, who have worked so hard to build the brand into what it is today and will continue to do their best to take the brand to the next level, year in, year out. I wish the brand all the success in the world. Go get them, Tiger!

. time for a **TIGE**